Francis Parkman

The Book of Roses

Francis Parkman

The Book of Roses

ISBN/EAN: 9783744689373

Printed in Europe, USA, Canada, Australia, Japan

Cover: Foto ©Thomas Meinert / pixelio.de

More available books at **www.hansebooks.com**

THE BOOK OF ROSES.

BY

FRANCIS PARKMAN.

BOSTON:
J. E. TILTON AND COMPANY.
1866.

STEREOTYPED BY C. J. PETERS & SON.

PRESS OF GEO. C. RAND & AVERY.

TO

EDWARD SPRAGUE RAND, JR.,

A HORTICULTURIST

WHOSE ENERGY AND SKILL

HAVE MADE

"*A WILDERNESS TO BLOSSOM AS THE ROSE*,"

THIS BOOK

IS CORDIALLY INSCRIBED.

CONTENTS.

	PAGE
INTRODUCTION	9

PART I.—CULTURE OF THE ROSE.

CHAP. I.—OPEN-AIR CULTURE.

PLANTING	16
PRUNING	17
CLIMBING AND PILLAR ROSES	21
SUBSEQUENT CULTURE	24
AN EXPERIMENT IN ROSE-GROWING	24
STANDARD ROSES	26
A NOVELTY IN ROSE CULTURE	28
ANOTHER NOVELTY	30
ENEMIES OF THE ROSE	32

CHAP. II.—POT CULTURE.

A NEW METHOD	46
FORCING	48
CHEAP FORCING	51
RAISING SPECIMEN ROSES	52

CHAP. III.—PROPAGATION.

LAYERS	59
CUTTINGS	62
BUDDING	67
GRAFTING	74
SUCKERS	76

CHAP. IV.—MISCELLANEOUS OPERATIONS.

RAISING NEW VARIETIES	76
IMPROVEMENT OF CLIMBING ROSES	87
NATURAL STANDARDS	88
EFFECTS OF FROST ON SOIL	89
GROUPING OF ROSES	90

PART II.—DESCRIPTION OF THE ROSE.

PAGE

CHAP. V.—GROUPS AND FAMILIES 95

CHAP. VI.—SUMMER ROSES.

    THE PROVENCE ROSE 111
    THE MOSS ROSE 113
    THE DAMASK ROSE 120
    THE ALBA ROSE 122
    THE FRENCH ROSE 123
    THE HYBRID CHINESE ROSE 126
    THE SCOTCH ROSE 132
    THE AUSTRIAN BRIER 134
    THE DOUBLE YELLOW ROSE 136
    THE SWEET-BRIER 140
    THE BOURSAULT ROSE 141
    THE AYRSHIRE ROSE 142
    THE EVERGREEN ROSE 145
    THE MULTIFLORA ROSE 149
    HYBRID CLIMBING ROSES 151
    THE BANKSIA ROSE 152
    THE PRAIRIE ROSE 155

CHAP. VII.—AUTUMNAL ROSES.

    THE CHINESE ROSE 161
    THE TEA-SCENTED ROSE 166
    THE MUSK ROSE 170
    THE NOISETTE ROSE 171
    THE DAMASK PERPETUAL ROSE 175
    THE BOURBON ROSE 179
    THE HYBRID PERPETUAL ROSE 183
    THE MACARTNEY ROSE 195
    THE CHEROKEE ROSE 196
    THE SMALL-LEAVED ROSE 197
    THE PERPETUAL MOSS ROSE 198
    THE PERPETUAL SCOTCH ROSE 199

SUPPLEMENT.

    ADDITIONAL SELECTED ROSES 201

INTRODUCTION

IT IS needless to eulogize the Rose. Poets from Anacreon and Sappho, and earlier than they, down to our own times, have sung its praises; and yet the rose of Grecian and of Persian song, the rose of troubadours and minstrels, had no beauties so resplendent as those with which its offspring of the present day embellish our gardens. The "thirty sorts of rose," of which John Parkinson speaks in 1629, have multiplied to thousands. New races have been introduced from China, Persia, Hindostan, and our own country; and these, amalgamated with the older families by the art of the hybridist, have produced still other forms of surpassing variety and beauty. This multiplication and improvement are still in progress. The last two or three years have been prolific beyond precedent in new roses; and, with all regard for old favorites, it cannot be denied, that, while a few of the roses of our forefathers still hold their ground, the greater part are cast into the shade by the brilliant products of this generation.

In the production of new roses, France takes the lead. A host of cultivators great and small — Laffay, Vibert, Verdier, Margottin, Trouillard, Portemer, and numberless others — have devoted themselves to the pleasant art of intermarrying the various families and individual varieties of the rose, and raising from them seedlings whose numbers every year may be counted by hundreds of thousands. Of these, a very few only are held worthy of preservation; and all the rest are consigned to the rubbish heap. The English, too, have of late done much in raising new varieties; though their climate is less favorable than that of France, and their cultivators less active and zealous in the work. Some excellent roses, too, have been produced in America. Our climate is very favorable to the raising of seedlings, and far more might easily be accomplished here.

In France and England, the present rage for roses is intense. It is stimulated by exhibitions, where nurserymen, gardeners, landed gentlemen, and reverend clergymen of the Established Church, meet in friendly competition for the prize. While the French excel all others in the production of new varieties, the English are unsurpassed in the cultivation of varieties already known; and nothing can exceed the beauty and perfection of some of the specimens exhibited at their innumerable rose-shows. If the severity of our climate has its disadvantages, the clearness of our air and the warmth of our summer sun more than counterbalance them; and it is certain that roses can be raised here in as high perfection, to say the very least, as in any part of Europe.

The object of this book is to convey information. The earlier portion will describe the various processes of culture, training, and propagation, both in the open ground and in pots; and this will be followed by an account of the various families and groups of the rose, with descriptions of the best varieties belonging to each. A descriptive list will be added of all the varieties, both of old roses and those most recently introduced, which are held in esteem by the experienced cultivators of the present day. The chapter relating to the classification of roses, their family relations, and the manner in which new races have arisen by combinations of two or more old ones, was suggested by the difficulties of the writer himself at an early period of his rose studies. The want of such explanations, in previous treatises, has left their readers in a state of lamentable perplexity on a subject which might easily have been made sufficiently clear.

Books on the rose, written for the climates of France or England, will, in general, greatly mislead the cultivators here. Extracts will, however, be given from the writings of the best foreign cultivators, in cases where experience has shown that their directions are applicable to the climate of the Northern and Middle States. The writer having been for many years a cultivator of the rose, and having carefully put in practice the methods found successful abroad, is enabled to judge with some confidence of the extent to which they are applicable here, and to point out exceptions and modifications demanded by the nature of our climate.

Among English writers on the rose, the best are Paul, Rivers, and more recently Cranston, together with the vivacious Mr. Radclyffe, a clergyman, a horticulturist, an excellent amateur of the rose, and a very amusing contributor to the "Florist." In France, Deslongchamps and several able contributors to the "Revue Horticole" are the most prominent. From these sources the writer of this book drew the instructions and hints which at first formed the basis of his practice; but he soon found that he must greatly modify it in accordance with American necessities. There was much to be added, much to be discarded, and much to be changed; and the results to which he arrived are given, as compactly as possible, in the following pages.

Jan. 1, 1866.

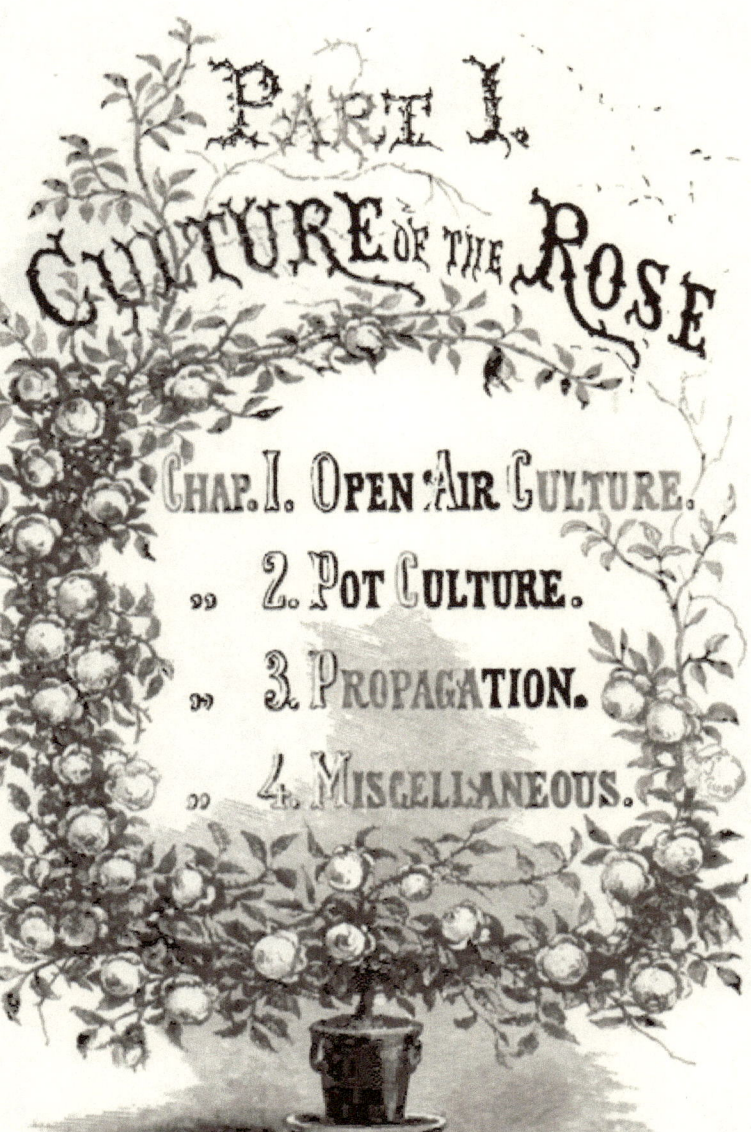

PART I.
CULTURE OF THE ROSE

Chap. 1. Open Air Culture.
,, 2. Pot Culture.
,, 3. Propagation.
,, 4. Miscellaneous.

OPEN AIR CULTURE

CHAP. I.

THE ROSE requires high culture. This belle of the parterre, this "queen of flowers," is a lover of rich fare, and refuses to put forth all her beauties on a meagre diet. Roses, indeed, will grow and bloom in any soil; but deficient nourishment will reduce the size of the flowers, and impair the perfection of their form. Of all soils, one of a sandy or gravelly nature is the worst; while, on the other hand, a wet and dense clay is scarcely better. A rich, strong, and somewhat heavy garden loam, abundantly manured, is the soil best adapted to all the strong-growing roses; while those of more delicate growth prefer one proportionably lighter.

Yet roses may be grown to perfection in any soil, if the

needful pains are taken. We will suppose an extreme case: The grower wishes to plant a bed of roses on a spot where the soil is very poor and sandy. Let him mark out his bed, dig the soil to the depth of eighteen inches, throw out the worst portion of it, and substitute in its place a quantity of strong, heavy loam: rotted sods, if they can be had, will be an excellent addition; and so, also, will decayed leaves. Then add a liberal dressing of old stable manure: that taken from a last year's hot-bed will do admirably. It is scarcely possible to enrich too highly. One-fourth manure to three-fourths soil is not an excessive proportion. Now incorporate the whole thoroughly with a spade, level the top, and your bed is ready.

Again: we will suppose a case, equally bad, but of the opposite character. Here the soil is very wet, cold, and heavy. The first step is to drain it. This may be done thoroughly with tiles, after the approved methods; or, if this is too troublesome or expensive, simpler means may be used, which will, in most situations, prove as effectual. Dig a hole about five feet deep and four feet wide at the lower side of your intended bed of roses: in this hole place an inverted barrel, with the head knocked out; or, what is better, an old oil cask. In the latter case, a hole should be bored in it, near the top, to permit the air to escape. Fill the space around the cask or barrel with stones, and then cover the whole with earth. If your bed is of considerable extent, a drain, laid in stone or tile, should be made under or beside the bed, at the depth of three feet, and so constructed as to lead to the sunken barrel. Throw out, if necessary, a portion of the worst soil of the bed, substituting light loam, rotted leaves, and coarse gritty sand. Then add an abundance of old stable manure, as in the former case.

In the great majority of gardens, however, such pains are superfluous. Any good garden soil, deeply dug, and thoroughly enriched, will grow roses in perfection. Neither manure nor the spade should be spared. Three conditions are indispensable, — sun, air, and exemption from the invasion of the roots of young growing trees. These last are insidious plunderers and thieves, which invade the soil, and rob its lawful occupants of the stores of nutriment provided for them.

A rose planted on the shady side of a grove of elm or maple trees is in one of the worst possible of situations. If, however, the situation is in other respects good, the evil of the invading roots may be cured for a time by digging a trench, three feet deep, between the trees and the bed of roses; thus cutting off the intruders. The trench may then be filled up immediately; but, if the trees are vigorous, it must be dug over again the following year. It is much better to choose, at the outset, an airy, sunny situation, at a reasonable distance from growing trees; but, at the same time, a spot exposed to violent winds should be avoided, as they are very injurious and exhausting.

PLANTING

Roses may be planted either in spring or in autumn. In the Northern States, the severity of the winter demands some protection, when planted in autumn, for all except the old, hardy varieties. Plant as early as possible, that the roots may take some hold on the soil before winter closes. October, for this reason, is better than November. The best protection is earth heaped around the stem to the height of from six inches to a foot. Pine, cedar, or spruce boughs are also excellent. When earth alone is used, the top of the rose is often frost-killed; but this is usually of no consequence, the growth and bloom being only more vigorous for this natural pruning. Dry leaves heaped among or around the roses, and kept down by sticks or pieces of board, or by earth thrown on them, are also good protectors. In spring, plant as early as the soil is in working order; that is to say, as soon as it is dry enough not to adhere in lumps to the spade.

In planting, prune back the straggling roots with a sharp knife, but save as many of the small fibres as possible. If you plant in spring, prune back the stem at least half way to the ground; but, if you plant in autumn, by all means defer this operation till the winter is over. The ground around autumn-planted roses should be trodden down in the spring, since the plant will have been somewhat loosened in its place by the effect of frost; but this treading must not take place until the soil has become free from excessive moisture. Budded roses require a peculiar treatment in planting, which we shall describe when we come to speak of them.

PRUNING

Next to soil and situation, pruning is the most important point of attention to the rose-grower. Long treatises have been written on it, describing in detail different modes applicable to different classes of roses, and confusing the amateur by a multitude of perplexing particulars. One principle will cover most of the ground: *Weakly-*

growing roses should be severely pruned: those of vigorous growth should be pruned but little. Or, to speak more precisely, *roses should be pruned in inverse proportion to the vigor of their growth.*

Much, however, depends on the object at which the grower aims. If he wishes for a profusion of bloom, without regard to the size and perfection of individual flowers, then comparatively little pruning is required. If, on the other hand, he wishes for blooms of the greatest size and perfection, without regard to number, he will prune more closely.

The pruning of any tree or shrub at a time when vegetation is dormant acts as a stimulus to its vital powers. Hence, when it is naturally vigorous, it is urged by close pruning to such a degree of growth, that it has no leisure to bear flowers, developing instead a profusion of leaves and branches. The few flowers which it may produce under such circumstances, will, however, be unusually large.

The most **vigorous** growers among roses are the climbers, such as the "Boursaults" and the "Prairies." These require very little pruning: first, because of their vigor; and, secondly, because quantity rather than quality of bloom is asked of them. The old and dry wood should be cut wholly away, leaving the strong young growth to take its place, with no other pruning than a clipping-off of the ends of side-shoots, and a thinning-out of crowded or misshapen branches. In all roses, it is the young, well-ripened wood that bears the finest flowers. Old enfeebled wood, or unripe, soft, and defective young wood, should always be removed.

Next in vigor to the climbers are some of the groups of hardy June roses; such, for example, as those called the Hybrid China roses. These are frequently grown on posts or pillars; in which case they require a special treatment, to be indicated hereafter. We are now supposing them to be grown as bushes in the garden or on the lawn. Cut out the old wood, and the weak, unripe, and sickly shoots, as well as those which interfere with others; then shorten the remaining stems one-third, and cut back the side-shoots to three or four buds. This is on the supposition that a full mass of bloom is required, without much regard to the development of individual flowers. If quality rather than quantity of bloom is the desideratum, the pruning both of the main stems and of the side-shoots must be considerably shorter.

Roses of more moderate growth, including the greater part of the June, Moss, Hybrid Perpetual, and Bourbon roses, require a proportionably closer pruning. The stems may be cut down to half their length, and the side-shoots shortened to two buds. All the weak-growing roses, of whatever class, may be pruned with advantage even more closely than this. Some of the weak-growing Hybrid Perpetuals grow and bloom best when shortened to within four or five buds of the earth. The strong-growing kinds, on the contrary, if pruned thus severely, would grow with great vigor, but give very few flowers.

The objects of pruning are threefold: first, to invigorate the plant; secondly, to improve its flowers; and, thirdly, to give it shape and proportion. This last object should always be kept in view by the operator. No two stems should be allowed to crowd each other. A mass of matted foliage is both injurious and unsightly. Sun and air should have access to every part of the plant. Six or seven stems are the utmost that should be allowed to remain, even on old established bushes; and these, as before mentioned, should be strong and well ripened, and should also be disposed in such a manner, that, when the buds have grown into shoots and leaves, the bush will have a symmetrical form. In young bushes, three, or even two, good stems are sufficient.

Pruning in summer, when the plant is in active

growth, has an effect contrary to that of pruning when it is in a dormant state. Far from increasing its vigor, it weakens it, by depriving it of a portion of its leaves, which are at once its stomach and its lungs. Only two kinds of summer pruning can be recommended. The first consists in the removal of small branches which crowd their neighbors, and interfere with them: the second is confined to the various classes of Perpetual roses, and consists merely in cutting off the faded flowers, together with the shoots on which they grow, to within three or four buds of the main stem. This greatly favors their tendency to bloom again later in the summer.

When old wood is cut away, it should be done cleanly, without leaving a protruding stump. A small saw will sometimes be required for this purpose; though in most cases a knife, or, what is more convenient, a pair of sharp pruning-shears, will be all that the operator requires.

CLIMBING AND PILLAR ROSES.

When roses are trained to cover walls, trellises, arches, or pillars, the main stems are encouraged to a strong growth. These form the permanent wood; while the sideshoots, more or less pruned back, furnish the flowers. For arbors, walls, or very tall pillars, the strongest growers are most suitable, such as the Prairie, Boursault, and Ayrshire roses. Enrich the soil strongly, and dig deep and widely. Choose a healthy young rose, and, in planting, cut off all the stems close to the earth. During the season, it will make a number of strong young shoots. In the following spring cut out half of them, leaving the strongest, which are to be secured against the wall, or over the arbor, diverging like a fan or otherwise, as fancy may suggest. The subsequent pruning is designed chiefly to regulate the growth of the rose, encouraging the progress of the long leading shoots until they have reached the required height, and removing side-shoots where they are too thick. Where a vacant space occurs, a strong neighboring shoot may be pruned back in spring to a single eye. This will stimulate it to a vigorous growth, producing a stem which will serve to fill the gap. Of the young shoots, which, more or less, will rise every season from the root, the greater part should be cut away, reserving two or three to take the place of the old original stems when these become weak by age. When these climbing roses are used for pillars, they may either be trained vertically, or wound in a spiral form around the supporting column.

Roses of more moderate growth are often trained to

poles or small pillars from six to twelve feet high. Some of the Hybrid China roses are, as before mentioned, well adapted to this use; and even some of the most vigorous Moss roses, such as *Princess Adelaide*, may be so trained. Where a pole is used, two stems are sufficient. These should be examined, and cut back to the first strong and plump bud, removing the weaker buds always found towards the extremity of a stem. Then let the stems so pruned lie flat on the earth till the buds break into leaf, after which they are to be tied to the pole. If they were tied up immediately, the sap, obeying its natural tendency, would flow upward, expanding the highest bud, and leaving many of those below dormant, so that a portion of the stem would be bare. (The same course of proceeding may be followed with equal advantage in the case of wall and trellis roses.) The highest bud now throws up a strong leading shoot, while the stem below becomes furnished with an abundance of small side-shoots. In the following spring, the leading shoot is to be pruned back to the first strong bud, and the treatment of the previous year repeated. By pursuing this process, the pillar may, in the course of two or three years, be enveloped from the ground to the summit with a mass of leaves and blossoms.

These and all other rose-pruning operations are, in the

Northern States, best effected in March, or the end of February; since roses pruned in autumn are apt to be severely injured and sometimes killed by the severity of our winters.

SUBSEQUENT CULTURE

Nothing is more beneficial to roses than a frequent digging and stirring of the soil around them. The surface should never be allowed to become hard, but should be kept light and porous by hoeing or forking several times in the course of the season. A yearly application of manure will be of great advantage. It may be applied in the autumn or in the spring, and forked in around the plants. Cultivators who wish to obtain the finest possible blooms sometimes apply liquid manure early in the summer, immediately after the flower-buds are formed. This penetrates at once to the roots, and takes immediate effect on the growing bud.

AN EXPERIMENT IN ROSE GROWING

The amateur may perhaps draw some useful hints from an experiment made by the writer in cultivating roses, with a view to obtaining the best possible individual flowers. A piece of land about sixty feet long by forty wide was "trenched" throughout to the depth of two feet and a half, and enriched with three layers of manure. The first was placed at eighteen inches from the surface; the second, at about nine inches; and the third was spread on the surface itself, and afterwards dug in. The virgin soil was a dense yellow loam of considerable depth; and, by the operation of "trenching," it was thoroughly mixed and incorporated with the black surface soil. Being too stiff and heavy, a large quantity of sandy road-scrapings was laid on with the surface-dressing of manure. When the ground was prepared, the roses were planted in rows. They consisted of Hardy June, Moss, Hybrid Perpetual, Bourbon, and a few of the more hardy Noisette roses. They were planted early in spring, and cut back at the same time close to the ground. Many of the Perpetuals and Bourbons flowered the first season, and all grew with a remarkable vigor. In November, just before the ground froze, a spadesman, working backward midway between the rows, dug a trench of the depth and width of his spade, throwing the earth in a ridge upon the roots of the roses as he proceeded. This answered a double purpose. The ridge of earth protected the roots and several inches of the stems, while the trench acted as a drain. In the spring, the earth of the ridge was drawn back into the trench with a hoe, and the roses pruned with great severity; some of the weak-growing Perpetuals and Mosses being cut to within two inches of the earth, and all the weak and sickly stems removed altogether. The whole ground was then forked over. The bloom was abundant, and the flowers of uncommon size and symmetry. Had the pruning been less severe, the mass of bloom would have been greater, but the individual flowers by no means of so good quality.

Standard Roses

Of budded roses we shall speak hereafter, in treating of propagation. There is one kind, however, which it will be well to notice here. In England and on the Continent, it is a common practice to bud roses on tall stems or standards of the Dog Rose, or other strong stock, sometimes at a height of five feet or more from the ground. The head of bloom thus produced has a very striking effect, especially when the budded rose is of a variety with long slender shoots, adapted to form what is called a "weeper."

In France, standard roses are frequently planted near together in circular or oval beds, the tallest stems being in the centre, and the rest diminishing in regular gradation to the edge of the bed, which is surrounded with dwarf roses. Thus a mound or hill of bloom is produced with a very striking and beautiful effect.

Unfortunately, the severe cold and sudden changes of the Northern States, and especially of New England, are very unfavorable to standard roses. The hot sun scorches and dries the tall, bare stem; and the sharp cold of winter frequently kills, and in almost every case greatly injures, the budded rose at the top. It is only by using great and very troublesome precaution that standards can here be kept in a thriving condition. This may be done most effectually by cutting or loosening the roots on one side, laying the rose flat on the ground, and covering it during winter under a ridge of earth. Some protection of the stem from the hot sun of July and August can hardly be dispensed with.

With regard to the mounds of standard roses first mentioned, it is scarcely worth while to attempt them here; but a very good substitute is within our reach. By choosing roses with a view to their different degrees of vigor, — planting the tall and robust kinds in the middle, and those of more moderate growth in regular gradation around them, — we may imitate the French mounds without the necessity of employing standards. Of course it will require time, and also judicious pruning, to perfect such a bed of roses; but, when this is done, it will be both a beautiful and permanent ornament of the lawn or garden.

A Novelty in Rose Culture.

A new mode of growing roses, so as to form a tall pyramid instead of a standard, has been recently introduced in England. Instead of inserting buds at the top of the stem only, they are inserted at intervals throughout its whole length, thus clothing it with verdure and flowers. By this means it is effectually protected from the sun, and one of the dangers which in our climate attend standard roses is averted. The following directions are copied from a late number of the "Gardener's Chronicle:" —

"Some strong two-years-old stocks of the Manetti Rose should be planted in November, in a piece of ground well exposed to sun and air. The soil should have dressings of manure, and be stirred to nearly two feet in depth. In the months of July and August of the following year, they will be in a fit state to bud. They should have one bud inserted in each stock close to the ground. The sort to be chosen for this preliminary budding is a very old Hybrid China Rose, called Madame Pisaroni; a rose with a most vigorous and robust habit, which, budded on strong Manetti stocks, will often make shoots from six to seven feet in length, and stout and robust in proportion. In the month of February following, the stocks in which are live buds should be all cut down to within six inches of the bud. In May, the buds will begin to shoot vigorously: if there are more shoots than one from each bud, they must be removed, leaving only one, which in June should be supported with a slight stake, or the wind may displace it.

"By the end of August, this shoot ought to be from five to six feet in height, and is then in a proper state for budding to form a pyramid. Some of the most free-growing and beautiful of the Hybrid Perpetual roses should be selected, and budded on these stems in the following manner: Commence about nine inches from the ground, inserting one bud; then on the opposite side of the stock, and at the same distance from the lower bud, insert another; and then at the same distance another and another; so that buds are on all sides of the tree up to about five feet in height, which, in the aggregate, may amount to nine buds. You will thus have formed the foundation of a pyramid. I need scarcely add that the shoots from the stock must be carefully removed during the growing season, so as to throw all its strength into the buds. It will also be advisable to pinch in the three topmost buds rather severely the first season, or they will, to use a common expression, draw up the sap too rapidly, and thus weaken the lower buds. In the course of a year or two, magnificent pyramids may thus be formed, their stems completely covered with foliage, and far surpassing any thing yet seen in rose culture."

Another new method of culture is put forward in recent French and English journals, and is said to have proved very successful, increasing both the size of the flowers and the period of bloom. I cannot speak of it from trial; but, as it may be found worth an experiment, I extract from the "Florist and Pomologist" the account there given of the process by a Mr. Perry, who was one of the first to practise it. He says,—

"As I have now spoken of the advantages attendant upon this mode of training, I will proceed to explain the method of carrying it out. I will suppose that the plants are well established, and are either on their own roots, or budded low on the Manetti (the former I prefer). The operation of bending and pegging-down should be performed in the month of March, or early in April. All the small growth should be cut clean away, and the ends of the strong shoots cut off to the extent only of a few inches. These shoots should then be carefully bent to the ground, and fastened down by means of strong wooden pegs, sufficiently stout to last the season, and to retain the branches in their proper positions. Care must be taken that the branches do not split off at the base; but the operator will soon perceive which is the best and easiest mode of bending the tree to his wishes. Many shoots will spring up from the base of the plants, too strong to produce summer blooms; but most of them will gratify the cultivator with such noble flowers in the autumn that will delight the heart of any lover of this queen of flowers. These branches will be the groundwork for the next year. I have recently been engaged in cutting all the old wood away which last season did such good duty, and am now furnished with an ample supply of shoots from four to eight feet high, which, if devoid of leaves, would strongly remind me of fine raspberry-canes, and which, by their appearance, promise what they will do for the forthcoming season. I would suggest that these long shoots should now be merely bundled together, and a stake put to each plant, so as to prevent their being injured by the wind. In this state let them remain until the latter end of March, and then proceed as I have before mentioned. I feel convinced, that, when this method of pegging-down and dwarfing strong-growing roses becomes generally known, many of the justly esteemed and valuable robust show varieties will occupy the position in our flower-gardens they are justly entitled to."

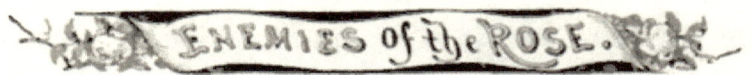

ENEMIES OF THE ROSE.

A good soil, a good situation, free air and full sun, joined with good manuring, good pruning, and good subsequent culture, will prevent more diseases than the most skilful practitioner would ever be able to cure. There are certain diseases, however, to which roses, under the best circumstances, are more or less liable. Of these, the most common, and perhaps the worst, is mildew. It consists in the formation on the leaves and stems of a sort of minute fungus, sometimes presenting the appearance of a white frost. Though often thought to be the result of dampness, it frequently appears in the dryest weather. Many of the Bourbon roses, and those of the Hybrid Perpetuals nearest akin to the Bourbons, are peculiarly liable to it. In the greenhouse, the best remedy is sulphur, melted and evaporated at a heat not high enough to cause it to burn. In the open air, the flour of sulphur may be sifted over the diseased plants. English florists use a remedy against mildew and other kinds of fungus, which is highly recommended, but of which I cannot speak from trial. It consists in syringing the plants affected with a solution of two ounces of blue vitriol dissolved in a large stable bucket of water.

The worst enemies of the rose belong to the insect world. Of these there are four, which, in this part of the country, cause far more mischief than all the rest combined. The first is the aphis, or green fly; the second is the rose-slug, or larva of the saw-fly; the third is the leaf-hopper, sometimes called the thrip; and the fourth is the small beetle, popularly called the rose-bug. The first three are vulnerable, and can be got rid of by using the right means. The slug is a small, green, semi-transparent grub, which appears on the leaves of the rose about the middle of June, eats away their vital part, and leaves nothing but a brown skeleton, till at length the whole bush looks as if burned. The aphis clings to the ends of young shoots, and sucks out their sap. It is prolific beyond belief, and a single one will soon increase to thousands. Both are quickly killed by a solution of whale-oil soap, or a strong decoction of tobacco, which should be applied with a syringe in the morning or evening, as the application of any liquid to the leaves of a plant under the hot sun is always injurious. The same remedy will kill the leaf-hopper, which, being much more agile than the others, is best assailed on a cold day, when its activity is to some degree chilled out of it. Both sides of the leaves should be syringed, and the plant thoroughly saturated with the soap or tobacco-water.

Two thorough and well-timed applications will suffice to destroy the year's crop of slugs.

The rose-bug is endowed with a constitution which defies tobacco and soap; and, though innumerable remedies have been proposed, we know no better plan than to pick them off the bushes by hand, or, watching a time when they are chilled with cold, to shake them off upon a cloth laid on the ground beneath. In either case, sure work should be made of them by scalding or crushing them to death.

The following account of the rose-bug and the slug is from Dr. Harris's work on "Insects Injurious to Vegetation:"—

"The saw-fly of the rose, which, as it does not seem to have been described before, may be called *Selandria Rosæ*, from its favorite plant, so nearly resembles the slug-worm saw-fly as not to be distinguished therefrom except by a practised observer. It is also very much like *Selandria barda*, *Vitis*, and *pygmæa*, but has not the red thorax of these three closely-allied species. It is of a deep and shining black color. The first two pairs of legs are brownish-gray, or dirty white, except the thighs, which are almost entirely black. The hind legs are black, with whitish knees. The wings are smoky and transparent, with dark-brown veins, and a brown spot near the middle of the edge of the first pair. The body of the male is a little more than three-twentieths of an inch long; that of the female, one-fifth of an inch or more; and the wings expand nearly or quite two-fifths of an inch. These saw-flies come out of the ground at various times between the 20th of May and the middle of June, during which period they pair, and lay their eggs. The females do not fly much, and may be seen, during most of the day, resting on the leaves; and, when touched, they draw up their legs, and fall to the ground. The males are now active, fly from one rose-bush to another, and hover around their sluggish partners. The latter, when about to lay their eggs, turn a little on one side, unsheathe their saws, and thrust them obliquely into the skin of the leaf, depositing in each incision thus made a single egg. The young begin to hatch in ten days or a fortnight after the eggs are laid. They may sometimes be found on the leaves as early as the 1st of June, but do not usually appear in considerable numbers till the 20th of the same month. How long they are in coming to maturity, I have not particularly observed; but the period of their existence in the caterpillar state probably does not exceed three weeks. They somewhat resemble young slug-worms in form, but are not quite so convex. They have a small, round, yellowish head, with a black dot on each side of it; and are provided with twenty-two short legs. The body is green above, paler at the sides, and yellowish beneath; and it is soft and almost transparent, like jelly. The skin of the back is transversely wrinkled, and covered with minute elevated points; and there are two small, triple-pointed warts on the edge of the first ring, immediately behind the head.

"The gelatinous and sluggish creatures eat the upper surface of the leaf in large, irregular patches, leaving the veins and the skin beneath untouched; and they are sometimes so thick, that not a leaf on the bushes is spared by them, and the whole foliage looks as if it had been scorched by fire, and drops off soon afterwards. They cast their skins several times, leaving them extended and fastened on the leaves: after the last moulting, they lose their semi-transparent and greenish color, and acquire an opaque yellowish hue. They then leave the rose-bushes; some of them slowly creeping down the stem, and others rolling up and dropping off, especially when the bushes are shaken by the wind. Having reached the ground, they burrow to the depth of an inch or more in the earth, where each one makes for itself a small oval cell of grains of earth, cemented with a little gummy silk. Having finished their transformations, and turned to flies within their cells, they come out of the ground early in August, and lay their eggs for a second brood of young. These, in turn, perform their appointed work of destruction in the autumn: they then go into the ground, make their earthen cells, remain therein throughout the winter, and appear in the winged form in the following spring and summer. During several years past, these pernicious vermin have infested the rose-bushes in the vicinity of Boston, and have proved so injurious to them as to have elicited the attention of the Massachusetts Horticultural Society, by whom a premium of one hundred dollars, for the most successful mode of destroying these insects, was offered in the summer of 1840. In the year 1832, I first observed them in the gardens in Cambridge, and then made myself acquainted with their transformations. At that time they had not reached Milton, my former place of residence; and they did not appear in that place till six or seven years later. They now seem to be gradually extending in all directions; and an effectual method for preserving our roses from their attacks has become very desirable to all persons who set any value on this beautiful ornament of our gardens and shrubberies. Showering or syringing the bushes, with a liquor made by mixing with water the juice expressed from tobacco by tobacconists, has been recommended: but some caution is necessary in making this mixture of a proper strength; for, if too strong, it is injurious to plants; and the experiment does not seem, as yet, to have been conducted with sufficient care to insure safety and success. Dusting lime over the plants, when wet with dew, has been tried, and found of some use; but this and all other remedies will probably yield in efficacy to Mr. Haggerston's mixture of whale-oil soap and water, in the proportion of two pounds of the soap to fifteen gallons of water.

"Particular directions, drawn up by Mr. Haggerston himself, for the preparation and use of this simple and cheap application, may be found in the 'Boston Courier' for the 25th of June, 1841, and also in most of our agricultural and horticultural journals of the same time. The utility of this mixture has already been repeatedly mentioned in this treatise, and it may be applied in other cases with advantage. Mr. Haggerston finds that it effectually destroys many kinds of insects; and he particularly mentions plant-lice, red spiders, canker-worms, and a little jumping insect, which has lately been found quite as hurtful to rose-bushes as the slugs or young of the saw-fly. The little insect alluded to has been mistaken for a Thrips, or vine-fretter: it is, however, a leaf-hopper, or species of *Tettigonia*, and is described in a former part of this treatise.

"The rose-chafer, or rose-bug as it is more commonly and incorrectly called, is also a diurnal insect. It is the *Melolontha subspinosa* of Fabricius, by whom it was first described, and belongs to the modern genus *Macrodactylus* of Latreille. Common as this insect is in the vicinity of Boston, it is, or was a few years ago, unknown in the northern and western parts of Massachusetts, in New Hampshire, and in Maine. It may, therefore, be well to give a brief description of it. This beetle measures seven-twentieths of an inch in length. Its body is slender, tapers before and behind, and is entirely covered with very short and close ashen-yellow down; the thorax is long and narrow, angularly widened in the middle of each side, which suggested the name *subspinosa*, or somewhat spined; the legs are slender, and of a pale-red color; the joints of the feet are tipped with black, and are very long; which caused Latreille to call the genus *Macrodactylus;* that is, long toe, or long foot.

"The natural history of the rose-chafer, one of the greatest scourges with which our gardens and nurseries have been afflicted, was for a long time involved in mystery, but is at last fully cleared up. The prevalence of this insect on the rose, and its annual appearance coinciding with the blossoming of that flower, have gained for it the popular name by which it is here known. For some time after they were first noticed, rose-bugs appeared to be confined to their favorite, the blossoms of the rose; but within forty years they have prodigiously increased in number, have attacked at random various kinds of plants in swarms, and have become notorious for their extensive and deplorable ravages. The grape-vine, in particular, the cherry, plum, and apple trees, have annually suffered by their depredations: many other fruit-trees and shrubs, garden vegetables and corn, and even the trees of the forest and the grass of the fields, have been laid under contribution by these indiscriminate feeders, by whom leaves, flowers, and fruits are alike consumed. The unexpected arrival of these insects in swarms at their first coming, and their sudden disappearance at the close of their career, are remarkable facts in their history. They come forth from the ground during the second week in June, or about the time of the blossoming of the damask-rose, and remain from thirty to forty days. At the end of this period the males become exhausted, fall to the ground, and perish; while the females enter the earth, lay their eggs, return to the surface, and, after lingering a few days, die also.

"The eggs laid by each female are about thirty in number, and are deposited from one to four inches beneath the surface of the soil: they are nearly globular, whitish, and about one-thirtieth of an inch in diameter, and are hatched twenty days after they are laid. The young larvæ begin to feed on such tender roots as are within their reach. Like other grubs of the Scarabæians, when not eating they lie upon the side, with the body covered, so that the head and tail are nearly in contact: they move with difficulty on a level surface, and are continually falling over on one side or the other. They attain their full size in the autumn, being then nearly three-quarters of an inch long, and about an eighth of an inch in diameter. They are of a yellowish-white color, with a tinge of blue towards the hinder extremity, which is thick, and obtuse or rounded. A few short hairs are scattered on the surface of the body. There are six short legs; namely, a pair to each of the first three rings behind the head: and the latter is covered with a horny shell of a pale rust color. In October they descend below the reach of frost, and pass the winter in a torpid state. In the spring they approach towards the surface, and each one forms for itself a little cell of an oval shape by turning round a great many times, so as to compress the earth, and render the inside of the cavity hard and smooth. Within this cell the grub is transformed to a pupa during the month of May by casting off its skin, which is pushed downwards in folds from the head to the tail. The pupa has somewhat the form of the perfected beetle, but is of a yellowish-white color; its short, stump-like wings, its antennæ, and its legs, are folded upon the breast; and its whole body is enclosed in a thin film, that wraps each part separately. During the month of June, this filmy skin is rent: the included beetle withdraws from its body and its limbs, bursts open its earthen cell, and digs its way to the surface of the ground. Thus the various changes, from the egg to the full development of the perfected beetle, are completed within the space of one year.

"Such being the metamorphoses and habits of these insects, it is evident that we cannot attack them in the egg, the grub, or the pupa state: the enemy in these stages is beyond our reach, and is subject to the control only of the natural but unknown means appointed by the Author of Nature to keep the insect tribes in check. When they have issued from their subterranean retreats, and have congregated upon our vines, trees, and other vegetable productions, in the complete enjoyment of their propensities, we must unite our efforts to seize and crush the invaders. They must indeed be crushed, scalded, or burned, to deprive them of life; for they are not affected by any of the applications usually found destructive to other insects. Experience has proved the utility of gathering them by hand, or of shaking them or brushing them from the plants into tin vessels containing a little water. They should be collected daily during the period of their visitation, and should be committed to the flames, or killed by scalding water. The late John Lowell, Esq., states that, in 1823, he discovered on a solitary apple-tree the rose-bugs 'in vast numbers, such as could not be described, and would not be believed if they were described, or at least none but an ocular witness could conceive of their numbers. Destruction by hand was out of the question,' in this case. He put sheets under the tree, shook them down, and burned them.

"Dr. Green of Mansfield, whose investigations have thrown much light on the history of this insect, proposes protecting plants with millinet, and says that in this way only did he succeed in securing his grape-vines from depredation. His remarks also show the utility of gathering them. 'Eighty-six of these spoilers,' says he, 'were known to infest a single rose-bud, and were crushed with one grasp of the hand.' Suppose, as was probably the case, that one-half of them were females: by this destruction, eight hundred eggs, at least, were prevented from becoming matured. During the time of their prevalence, rose-bugs are sometimes found in immense numbers on the flowers of the common white-weed, or ox-eyed daisy (*Chrysanthemum leucanthemum*); a worthless plant, which has come to us from Europe, and has been suffered to overrun our pastures and encroach on our mowing-lands. In certain cases, it may become expedient rapidly to mow down the infested white-weed in dry pastures, and consume it, with the sluggish rose-bugs, on the spot.

"Our insect-eating birds undoubtedly devour many of these insects, and deserve to be cherished and protected for their services. Rose-bugs are also eaten greedily by domesticated fowls; and when they become exhausted and fall to the ground, or when they are about to lay their eggs, they are destroyed by moles, insects, and other animals, which lie in wait to seize them. Dr. Green informs us that a species of dragon-fly, or devil's-needle, devours them. He also says that an insect, which he calls the enemy of the cut-worm (probably the larva of a Carabus or predaceous ground-beetle), preys on the grubs of the common dor-bug. In France, the golden ground-beetle (*Carabus auratus*) devours the female dor, or chafer, at the moment when she is about to deposit her eggs. I have taken one specimen of this fine ground-beetle in Massachusetts; and we have several other kinds equally predaceous, which probably contribute to check the increase of our native Mclolonthians."

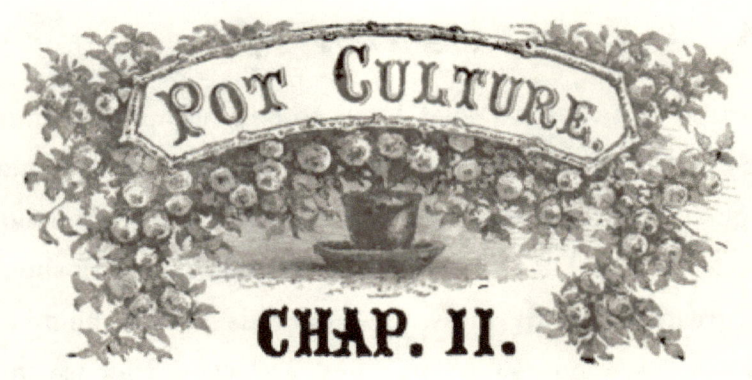

POT CULTURE.

CHAP. II.

MANY OF the ever-blooming roses cannot, in our climate, be cultivated in the open air without extreme precaution to protect them from the cold. To grow them most successfully, the aid of glass is necessary. Many of the Hardy Perpetual roses may also be grown with advantage in pots, by which means their bloom may be prolonged into the early winter months, or they may be forced into premature flowering long before their natural season of bloom. The first essential in the pot culture of roses is the preparation of the soil. Those of delicate growth, like most of the China and Tea roses, require a lighter soil than the more robust varieties, like most of the Hardy Perpetuals. A mixture of loam, manure, leaf-mould, and sand, in the proportion of two bushels of loam to one bushel of manure, one bushel of leaf-mould, and half a bushel of sand, makes a good soil for the more delicate roses. For the more robust kinds, the proportion of loam and of manure should be greater. In all cases, the materials should be mixed two or three months before they are wanted for use, and turned over several times to incorporate them thoroughly. They are frequently, however, mixed, and used at once. The best loam is that composed of thoroughly rotted turf. A very skilful English rose-grower, Mr. Rivers, recommends the compact turf shaved from the surface of an old pasture, and roasted and partially charred on a sheet of iron over a moderate fire. I have found no enriching material so good as the sweepings from the floor of a horse-shoer, in which manure is mixed with the shavings of hoofs. It is light and porous, and furnishes, in decomposing, a great quantity of ammonia. For the more delicate roses it is particularly suited, while the stronger kinds will bear manures of a stronger and denser nature. The light black soil from the woods is an excellent substitute for leaf-mould; or, to speak more correctly, it is a natural leaf-mould in the most thorough state of decomposition.

Young and thrifty roses which have been grown during summer may be potted for the house in September. They should be taken up with care, the large straggling roots cut back, and all bruised ends removed with a sharp knife. The ends of the branches should also be cut back. They may then be potted in the compost just described, which should first be sifted through a very coarse sieve. The pots must be well drained with broken crocks placed over the hole at the bottom. Care must be taken that the pot be not too large, as this is very injurious. A sharp stick may be used to compact the soil about the roots; and from half an inch to an inch in depth should be left empty at the top, to assist in thorough watering, which is a point of the first importance.

When the roses are potted, they should be placed in a light cellar or shed, or under a shady wall. They must be well watered, and it is well to syringe them occasionally. In a week or two they will have become established, and may then be removed to a greenhouse without fire, and with plenty of air; care, however, being taken to protect them from frost at night.

The roses so treated are intended for blooming from mid-winter to the end of spring; and we shall soon speak further of them under the head of Forcing.

A great desideratum is the obtaining of roses in the early part of winter. This may be done by growing ever-blooming roses in pots in the open air during summer, plunging the pot in the earth, and placing a tile or brick beneath it to prevent the egress of roots and the ingress of worms. Towards the end of August, cut off all the flowers and buds, at the same time shortening the flower-stalks to two or three eyes. Then give the roses a supply of manure-water to stimulate their growth. If they are in a thrifty condition, they will form new shoots and flower-buds before the frost sets in; and may then be removed to a cold greenhouse, where they will continue to flower for several months.

A New Method.

The following is the description given by Mr. Rivers of a practice recently introduced in England, and which seems well worth a trial here, with such modifications as the heat of our sun may require:—

"To have a fine bloom of these roses, or, indeed, of any of the Hybrid Perpetuals, Bourbons, or China roses, in pots towards the end of summer or autumn, take plants from small pots (those struck from cuttings in March or April will do), and put them into six-inch, or even eight-inch pots, using a compost of light turfy loam and rotten manure, equal parts: to a bushel of the compost add half a peck of pounded charcoal, and the same quantity of silver sand; make a hot-bed of sufficient strength, say three to four feet in height, of seasoned dung, so that it is not of a burning heat, in a sunny, exposed situation, and on this place the pots; then fill up all interstices with saw-dust, placing it so as to cover the rims, and to lie on the surface of the mould in the pots about two inches deep. The pots should have a good sound watering before they are thus plunged, and have water daily in dry weather. The bottom heat and full exposure to the sun and air will give the plants a vigor almost beyond belief. This very simple mode of culture is as yet almost unknown. I have circulated among a few friends the above directions; and have no doubt, that, in the hands of skilful gardeners, some extraordinary results may be looked for in the production of specimens of soft-wooded plants. I may add, that, when the heat of the bed declines towards the middle of July, the pots must be removed, some fresh dung added, and the bed remade, again plunging the plants immediately. Towards the end of August, the roots of the plants must be ripened: the pots must, therefore, be gradually lifted out of the saw-dust; i.e., for five or six days, expose them about two inches below their rims; then, after the same lapse of time, a little lower, till the whole of the pot is exposed to the sun and air: they may be then removed to the greenhouse, so as to be sheltered from heavy rain. They will bloom well in the autumn, and be in fine order for early forcing. If plants are required during the summer for exhibition, or any other purpose, care must always be taken to harden or ripen their roots, as above, before they are removed from the hot-bed."

"Forcing" is the very inappropriate name of the process by which roses and other plants are induced to bloom under glass in advance of their natural season. We say that the name is inappropriate, because one of the chief essentials to the success of the process consists in an abstinence from all that is violent or sudden, and in the gentle and graduated application of the stimulus of artificial heat.

Roses may be forced in the greenhouse, but not to advantage, because the conditions of success will be inconsistent with the requirements of many of the other plants. The process is best carried on in a small glass structure made for such purposes, and called a "forcing-pit."

A pit ten or twelve feet long and eight or ten wide will commonly be large enough. It may be of the simplest and cheapest construction. In a dry situation, there is advantage in sinking the lower part of it two or three feet below the surface of the ground. The roses may be placed on beds of earth, or on wooden platforms, so arranged as to bring the top of the plants near the glass; and a sunken path may pass down the middle. The pit may be heated by a stove enclosed with brick-work, and furnished with a flue of brick or tile passing along the front of the pit, and entering the chimney at the farther end. The lights must be movable, or other means provided for ample ventilation; and if these are such that the air on entering will pass over the heated flues, and thus become warmed in the passage, great advantage will result. A pit may be appended to a greenhouse; in which case it may be heated by hot-water pipes furnished with means of cutting off or letting on the water.

The roses potted for forcing, as directed in the last section, should be kept in a dormant state till the middle of December. A portion of them may then be brought into the pit, and the young shoots pruned back to two or three eyes. The heat at first must be very moderate, not much exceeding forty-five degrees in the daytime: and, throughout the process, the pit should be kept as cool as possible at night; great care, however, being taken that no frost is admitted. With this view, the glass should be covered at sunset with thick mats. Syringe the plants as the buds begin to swell, and lose no opportunity to give air on mild and bright days. Raise the heat gradually till it reaches sixty degrees; which is enough during the winter months, so far as fire-heat is concerned. The heat of the sun will sometimes raise it to seventy or eighty degrees. Syringe every morning; and, if the aphis appears, fumigate with tobacco; then syringe forcibly to wash off the dead insects. As the plants advance in growth, they require plenty of water; and, as the buds begin to swell, manure-water may be applied once or twice. When the buds are ready to open, the pots may be removed to the greenhouse or drawing-room, and another supply put in their place for a second crop of flowers. When the blooms are faded, the flower-stalks may be cut back to two or three eyes, and the plants placed again in the forcing-pit for another crop. This, of course, is applicable to ever-blooming roses only.

The most common and simple way, however, of obtaining roses in winter, is to grow them on rafters in the greenhouse. Some of the Noisette, China, and Tea roses, thus treated, will furnish an abundant supply of excellent flowers. By pruning them at different periods during the summer and autumn, they will be induced to flower in succession; since, with all roses, the time of blooming is, to a great degree, dependent on the time of pruning.

Roses potted in the manner described for forcing may also be brought into bloom in the sunny window of a chamber or drawing-room. They will bloom much better if allowed to remain at rest in a cool cellar for a month or two after potting.

Cheap Forcing

The following is a cheap mode of forcing, described by an English cultivator. The amateur may, perhaps, be disposed to make the experiment.

"Those who wish for the luxury of forced roses at a trifling cost may have them by pursuing the following simple method: Take a common garden frame, large or small, according to the number of roses wanted; raise it on some posts, so that the bottom edge will be about three feet from the ground at the back of the frame, and two feet in front, sloping to the south. If it is two feet deep, this will give a depth of five feet under the lights at the back of the frame, which will admit roses on little stems as well as dwarfs. Grafted or budded plants of any of the Perpetual roses should be potted in October, in a rich compost of equal portions of rotten dung and loam, in pots about eight inches deep and seven inches over, and plunged in the soil at the bottom. The air in the frame may be heated by linings of hot dung; but care must be taken that the dung be turned over two or three times before it is used, otherwise the rank and noxious steam will kill the young and tender shoots: but the hazard of this may be avoided by building a wall of turf, three inches thick, from the ground to the bottom edge of the frame. This will admit the heat through it, and exclude the steam. The Perpetual roses, thus made to bloom early, are really beautiful."

RAISING SPECIMEN ROSES

Now, in the way of exciting the reader's emulation, I will mention a few items of the opening flower-show of the Crystal Palace, Sydenham, on the 26th of May, a few years ago. The following specimens of roses, in pots, are chronicled among innumerable others:—

MADAME WILLERMOZ (*Tea-scented Rose*), seven feet high, with more than a hundred expanded flowers.

SOUVENIR DE LA MALMAISON (*Bourbon Rose*), with thirty expanded flowers, the largest more than five inches in diameter.

PAUL PERRAS (*Hybrid Bourbon Rose*), six feet high, with nearly a hundred expanded flowers.

COUPE D'HÉBÉ (*Hybrid Bourbon Rose*), six feet high, covered with a mass of bloom.

These were all raised by Mr. Paul, one of the most skilful

of English rose-growers; and were the results of patience, care, and experience. We hold the production of specimens like these a work of art worthy of zealous emulation. Our climate is quite as favorable to their production as that of England; and, when the floricultural art has reached among us the same development, our horticultural shows will, no doubt, boast decorations equally splendid. The plants just mentioned were the productions of a nurseryman; but specimens of roses grown to the highest perfection are every year exhibited in England by amateur cultivators. The competition for prizes, far from being a mere strife for a small sum of money, is an honorable emulation, in which the credit of success is the winner's best reward.

One point cannot be too often urged in respect to horticultural pursuits. Never attempt to do any thing which you are not prepared to do thoroughly. A little done well is far more satisfactory than a great deal done carelessly and superficially. He who raises one perfect and fully developed specimen of a plant is a better horticulturist than he who raises an acre of indifferent specimens. The amateur who has made himself a thorough master of the cultivation of a single species or variety, has, of necessity, acquired a knowledge and skill, which, with very little pains, he may apply to numberless other forms of culture. Learn to produce a first-class specimen of the rose grown in a pot, and you will have no difficulty in successfully applying your observation and experience to a vast variety of plants. We will, therefore, enter into some detail as to the methods of procedure. For many of the specific directions I am indebted to Mr. Paul, the exhibiter of the fine specimens named above, and the author, among other books, of a useful little treatise on the cultivation of roses in pots.

Soil is the point that first demands attention, and directions concerning it have already been given. You have bought a number of young roses, in small pots, in the spring. Be sure that these roses have been in a dormant state during the winter; for, if they have been kept in growth, their vital power is partially exhausted. They may be budded on short stems of the Manetti or other good stock (see the chapter on *Budding*), or they may be on their own roots. The Tea and China roses are certainly better in the latter condition. Shift them from the small pots into pots a very little larger, without breaking the ball of earth around their roots. Water them well, and plunge them to the edge of the pot in earth, in an open, airy, sunny place. Or they may be set on the surface, provided the spaces between them are well packed with tan, coal-ashes, or swamp-moss. The last is excellent: it holds moisture like a sponge. In every case, the pots should rest on flat bricks, slates, tiles, or inverted pans, in order that worms may be excluded, and that the roots may not be tempted to thrust themselves through the hole. In potting, thorough drainage should be secured by placing broken crocks at the bottom of the pot.

Encourage the growth of the plants by pinching off the flower-buds. The object throughout the summer is to get a few stout well-ripened shoots by autumn. Therefore the pots should not be very close together, since this would deprive the plants of free air and sunlight. Watering must be carefully attended to. Cut out, or pinch off, weak or ill-placed shoots; or, what is better, prevent their growth by rubbing off the buds that threaten to form such. Thus, if several buds are crowded together in one place, rub off all but one or two of them, choosing the strongest for preservation. This is called *dis-budding*. Those of the plants that grow most vigorously will require to be shifted into still larger pots in July; but this should be done only in cases where it is necessary. As a guide on this point, turn them carefully out of the pots to examine the roots; and, if these are found protruding in great abundance from the ball of earth, larger pots will be required; but, if otherwise, the same one will suffice. Some roses suffer greatly if placed in pots too large for them; and the same is more or less true of all plants.

Late in autumn, when growth has ceased, shift the roses again, if they need it, and place them for wintering in a cellar or cold frame. In the spring, prune them, as directed in the chapter on Pruning. After the rose is pruned, stake out the shoots to as great distances as possible. Indeed, the larger ones should be made to lie almost horizontal: this will cause the buds to "break," or open, regularly along their whole length; whereas, if left upright, a few at the top would break, and the rest remain dormant. As soon as the buds have opened, the shoots may be tied up again. Syringe the opening buds, and water moderately, increasing the amount of moisture as the leaves expand, and watering abundantly during all the period of full activity of growth; that is, during summer and early autumn. An occasional application of manure-water is useful. Watch for insects and mildew, and apply the remedies elsewhere directed. About midsummer, shift those that need it into larger pots; an operation which, if performed with skill, will not check their growth in the least. Continue to dis-bud and to remove weak and ill-placed shoots, tying out the rest, as they grow, to stakes, in order to bring the plant into a symmetrical form. This form is a matter of taste with the cultivator: it may be a half-globe, a fan, or a pyramid or cone. The last is usually the best; one strong stem being allowed to grow in the centre, and smaller stems trained in gradation around it. None must interfere with their neighbors, and air should have free play through the plant.

You have reached the second autumn, and your plants are now excellent for forcing; but, if you aim at first-class specimens, you must give them, at the least, one season more of growth and training. To this end, keep them dormant through the winter in a cellar or cold frame as before, and prune them early in spring. We will suppose that a pyramidal plant is desired. As soon as they are pruned, draw the lower shoots downwards over the rim of the pot, just beneath which a wire should pass around, to which the shoots are to be tied with strings of bass-matting. The shoots higher up are to be arranged, with the aid of sticks and strings, so as to decrease in circumference till they terminate in a point. Constant care and some judgment are needed throughout the growing season to preserve symmetry of form. Strong shoots must be pinched back, and weak ones encouraged. Both the plant, and the pot that contains it, are, or ought to be, so large by this time, that handling them, especially in the act of shifting, becomes somewhat difficult. In the third, or at farthest in the fourth autumn, you may expect, as the result of your pains, a plant that in its blooming season will make a brilliant contrast with the half-grown and indifferent specimens sometimes exhibited at our horticultural shows.

If you forget every other point of the above directions, keep in mind the following: Drain your pots thoroughly; and, when you water them, be sure that you give water enough to penetrate the whole mass of the earth contained in them. Watering only the surface, and leaving the roots dry, is ruinous.

PROPAGATION
CHAP. II.

THERE ARE five modes of propagating the rose, — by layers, by cuttings, by budding, by grafting, and by suckers.

LAYERS

This is perhaps, for the amateur, the most convenient and certain method. The best season for layering is the summer, from the end of June to the end of August; and, for some varieties, even later. The rose which is to be multiplied should be in a condition of vigorous growth. Loosen and pulverize the soil around it; and, if heavy and adhesive, add a liberal quantity of very old manure mixed with its bulk of sharp sand. The implements needed for the operation are a knife, a trowel, and hooked wooden pegs. Choose a well-ripened shoot of the same season's growth, and strip off the leaves from its base a foot or more up the stalk; but, by all means, suffer the leaves at the end to remain. Bend the shoot gently downward with the left hand, and insert the edge of the knife in its upper or inner side six or eight inches from its base, and immediately below a bud. Cut half way through the stem; then turn the edge of the knife upward, and cautiously slit the stem through the middle, to the length of an inch and a half: thus a tongue of wood, with a bud at its end, will be formed. With the thumb and finger of the left hand raise the upper part of the stem erect, at the same time by a slight twist turning the tongue aside, steadying the stem meanwhile with the right hand. Thus the tongue will be brought to a right angle, or nearly so, with the part of the stem from which it was cut. Hold it in this position with the left hand, while with the trowel you make a slit in the soil just beneath it. Into this insert the tongue and bent part of the stem to a depth not much exceeding two inches. Press the earth firmly round them, and pin them down with one of the hooked pegs. Some operators cut the tongue on the lower or outer side of the stem; but this has a double disadvantage. In the first place, the stem is much more liable to break in being bent; and, in the next place, the tongue is liable to re-unite with the cut part, and thus defeat the operation. When all is finished, the extremity of the shoot should stand out of the ground as nearly upright as possible, and should by no means be cut back,—a mistaken practice in use with some gardeners.

In a favorable season, most of the layers will be well rooted before the frost sets in. If the weather is very dry, there will be many failures. Instead of roots, a hard cellular substance will form in a ball around the tongue. In the dry summer of 1864, the rose-layers were thus "clubbed" with lumps often as large as a hen's egg; but cases like this are rare.

In November, it is better in our severe climate to take up the rooted layers, and keep them during winter in a "cold frame;" that is, a frame constructed like that of a hot-bed, without the heat. Here they should be set closely in light soil to the depth of at least six inches, and covered with boards and matting; or they may be potted in small pots, and placed in a frame or cellar.

Layers may be made in spring from wood of the last season's growth; but laying the young wood during summer, as described above, is much to be preferred.

CUTTINGS.

All roses may be propagated by cuttings; but some kinds strike root much more readily than others. The hard-wooded roses, including the entire family of the Hardy June roses, and especially the Mosses, are increased with difficulty by cuttings. The Hybrid Perpetuals root more readily; while the tender ever-blooming roses, including the Teas, Noisettes, and Chinas, are propagated in this way with great ease.

Cuttings may be made from the ripened or the half-ripened wood. In the case of roses, and of nearly all ligneous plants, cuttings made from the ripe wood do not require bottom-heat, and are more likely to be injured than benefited by it. On the other hand, cuttings of the soft or unripe wood strike root with more quickness and certainty if stimulated by the application of a gentle heat from below.

In propagating roses from the ripe wood, the cuttings must be made early in autumn from wood of the same season's growth. The chances of success will be increased if they are taken off close to the old wood with what is called a "heel;" that is, with a very small portion of the old wood attached. The heel should be trimmed smooth with a sharp knife: the cuttings may be six or eight inches long. Strip off any leaves which may still adhere to them, and plant them in rows, at a depth of about five inches, in a cold frame. The soil should be very light, and thoroughly drained: water it, to settle it, around the cuttings. On the approach of frost, they should be protected with boards and mats, giving them air on fine days during winter. In the spring, a white cellular growth called a "callus" will have formed at the heel of each cutting, which, if the process succeeds, will soon emit roots, and become a plant.

Propagation in summer from the half-ripe wood is a better and less uncertain method. In June and July, immediately after the blossoms wither, and before the rose has begun its second growth, cuttings should be made of the flower-stems. Each cutting may contain two or three buds. The lower leaves must be taken off; but the upper leaves must remain. Trim off the stem smoothly with a sharp knife below the lowest bud, and as near to it as possible without injuring it.

If the cuttings are taken off with a heel, as above described, the chance of success will be greater. They may now be inserted at the depth of an inch and a half around the edge of a small pot filled one-third with broken crocks, and the remainder with a mixture of loam, leaf-mould, and sharp sand. Now place them in a frame on the shady side of a hedge or fence, water them to settle the soil, and cover them closely with glass. Sprinkle them lightly every morning and night; and, when moisture gathers on the inner surface of the glass, turn it over, placing the dry side inward. If mould or decay attacks the cuttings, wedge up the glass a little to give them air. In a week or two, they will form a callus; after which they may be removed to a gentle hot-bed, kept moderately close, and shaded from the direct sun. Here they will quickly strike root, and may be potted off singly into small pots.

Another mode of propagation, and a favorite one with nursery-men, is practised early in the spring. In this case, the cuttings are made from forced roses, or roses grown on greenhouse rafters. Some propagators prefer the wood in a very soft state, cutting it even before the flowers are expanded. The cuttings may be placed in pots as in the former case, or in shallow boxes or earthen pans thoroughly drained with broken crocks. The soil should be shallow enough to allow the heel of the cutting to touch the crocks. They are to be placed at once on a moderate bottom-heat, covered closely with glass, and shaded from the direct rays of the noontide sun. Their subsequent treatment is similar to that of summer cuttings. They must be closely watched, and those that show signs of mould or decay at once removed.

After the callus is formed, they will bear more air. When rooted, they should be potted into small pots, and placed on a hot-bed of which the heat is on the decline. Towards the end of May, when the earth is warmed by the sun, they may be turned out of the pots into the open ground, where they will soon make strong plants.

Many American nursery-men strike rose-cuttings in spring, in pure sand, over a hot-bed or a tank of hot water, in the close air of the propagating-house. They must be potted immediately on rooting, as the sand supplies them with nothing to subsist on. We have seen many hundreds rooted in this way with scarcely a single failure.

The management of difficult cuttings requires a certain tact, only to be gained by practice and observation; and the gardener who succeeds in rooting a pot of cuttings of the Moss Rose has some reason to be proud of his success.

With respect to the relative value of roses propagated by the methods above described, the most experienced cultivators are unanimous in the opinion, that those raised from layers and from cuttings of the ripe wood, without artificial heat, are superior in vigor and endurance to those raised from the half-ripe wood with the stimulus of a close heat. Unfortunately, the former method is so slow and uncertain when compared with the latter, that nurserymen rarely employ it to any great extent; and a good choice of roses on their own roots, raised without heat, is sometimes difficult to find.

The following is a mode of propagation not often practised, but which is well worthy of trial, as it is applicable to prunings which are usually thrown away. The extract is from the "Gardener's Chronicle."

"The rose is as easily propagated by means of buds or eyes as the vine. If your correspondent 'X' will take a strong shoot from almost any kind of rose in a dormant state, and with a sharp knife cut it into as many pieces as there are good eyes on the shoots, the pieces not being more than one inch long, taking care to have the eye in the centre of the piece, he will doubtless succeed. One-third of the wood should be cut clean off from end to end at the back of the eye, just as you would prepare a vine eye. In preparing the cutting-pans, it is most essential to put a good quantity of broken potsherds in the bottom, beginning with large pieces, and finishing with others more finely broken: then mix a quantity of good loam, leaf-soil, and sand, in equal proportions; rub it through a fine sieve, and fill the pans to within one inch of the top, pressing down the soil moderately firm. After that, put in the eyes in a leaning or slanting position, pressing them firmly into the soil with the thumb and finger; taking care to keep the thumb on the bottom end of the cutting, to prevent the bark from being injured. After the eyes are put in, give the pan two or three gentle raps on the bench; then put half an inch of silver or clean river sand on the top, water with a fine rose, and plunge the pans in a nice bottom heat of say sixty degrees, covering the surface over with moss to prevent the soil from getting dry: they will not require any more water for a week or ten days. The moss should be carefully removed as soon as the young shoots begin to push through the sand. In three weeks from that time, the roses will be fit for potting off into large sixty-sized pots. They should then be placed in a temperature of seventy degrees, when they will soon repay the care bestowed on them. I, however, prefer grafting on the Manetti stock. I grafted a lot in a dormant state seven weeks ago: they are now nice plants, and will be in bloom by May."—*J. Willis, Oulton Park, Cheshire.*

Budding.

This mode of propagation is attended with great advantages and great evils. A new or rare rose may be increased by it more rapidly and surely than by any other means; while roses of feeble growth on their own roots will often grow and bloom vigorously when budded on a strong and congenial stock. On the other hand, the very existence of a budded rose is, in our severe climate, precarious. A hard winter may kill it down to the point of inoculation, and it is then lost past recovery; whereas a rose on its own roots may be killed to the level of the earth, and yet throw up vigorous shoots in the spring. Moreover, a budded rose requires more attention than the cultivator is always willing to bestow on it. An ill-informed or careless amateur will suffer shoots to grow from the roots or stem of the stock; and, as these are always vigorous, they engross all the nourishment, and leave the budded rose to dwindle or die; while its disappointed owner, ignorant of the true condition of things, often congratulates himself on the prosperous growth of his plant. At length he is undeceived by the opening of the buds, and the appearance of a host of insignificant single roses in the place of the Giant of Battles or General Jacqueminot.

Budding, however, cannot be dispensed with, since, in losing it, we should lose the most effectual means of increasing and distributing the choicest roses. The process consists in implanting, as it were, an undeveloped leaf-bud, of the variety we wish to increase, in the bark and wood of some other species of rose. The latter is called the stock, and it should be of a hardy and vigorous nature. Two conditions are essential to the process. The first is, that the bark of the stock will "slip;" in other words, separate freely from the wood. The second is, that the rose to be increased should be furnished with young and sound leaf-buds in a dormant state. These conditions are best answered in summer and early autumn, from the first of July to the middle of September. During the whole of this period, the sap being in active motion, the bark separates freely from the wood, while there is always a supply of plump and healthy buds on shoots of the same year's growth. The only implement necessary is a budding-knife. The operator should also provide himself with strings of bass-matting, moistened to make them pliant. Instead of the bass, cotton-wicking is occasionally used. Cut well-ripened shoots of the variety to be increased, provided with plump and healthy buds. In order to prevent exhaustion by evaporation from the surface of the leaves, these should be at once cut off; leaving, however, about half an inch of the leaf-stalk still attached to the stem. Insert the knife in the bark of the stem half an inch above a bud, and then pass it smoothly downward to the distance of half an inch below the bud, thus removing the latter with a strip of bark attached. A small portion of the wood will also adhere. This may be removed; though this is not necessary, and is attended with some little risk of pulling out with it the eye, or vital part, of the bud. Now place the bud between the lips while you take the next step of the process. This consists in cutting a vertical slit in the bark of the stock. This done, cut a tranverse slit across the top of the vertical one. Both should be quite through the bark to the wood below; then, with the flat handle of the budding-knife, raise the corners of the bark, and disengage it from the wood sufficiently to allow of the bud being slipped smoothly into the crevice between the wood and bark of the stock. Next apply the edge of the knife to the protruding end of the bark attached to the bud, and cut it smoothly off immediately over the tranverse slit in the bark of the stock. The bud is now adjusted accurately in its place, the overlapping bark closing neatly around it. Now tie it above and below pretty firmly with repeated turns of the bass-matting, and the work is done. It must be remembered, that, to be well done, it must be quickly done; and it is better to insert the bud on the north or shady side of the stock.

The bud and the stock will soon begin to grow together. After a week or two they should be examined, and the tie loosened. If the bud is put in early in the season, it may be made to grow almost immediately by cutting off the ends of the growing shoots of the stock, and thus forcing sap towards the bud. As the bud grows, the stock should be still further shortened, and all the shoots growing below the bud should be removed altogether.

Budded stocks require in this country, at least when the buds are dormant, a protection against the winter. Where there are but few, oiled paper, or something of a similar nature, may be tied over the bud as a shelter from snow, rain, and sun; but, when there are many, this is impossible, and the stocks may be taken up, and "heeled" close together in a dry soil under a shelter of boards and mats. "Heeling" is merely a temporary planting.

In the following spring, the stocks may be cut off to within an inch of the bud, and then planted where they are to remain. When the bud is inserted near the ground, — which in our climate should always be done, — the stock should be planted in such a manner that the bud is a little below the level of the earth. To this end, the stock should be set in a slanting position in the hole dug for it; the bud, of course, being uppermost, and about an inch below the level of the edge of the hole: then the hole should be partially filled in. When the bud has grown out to the height of six or eight inches, the hole may be filled altogether. No part of the stock will now be seen above the earth. By this means, the point of junction of the stock and the bud is protected from the cold of winter and the heat of summer, and the rose will live longer and thrive better than where the stock is exposed. In many cases, the rose will throw out roots of its own above its junction with the stock, and thus become in time a self-rooted plant.

There are two kinds of stocks in common use at the present time for out-door roses. One is the Dog Rose, a variety growing wild in various parts of Europe; the other is the Manetti Rose, a seedling raised by the Italian cultivator whose name it bears. There can be no doubt, that, of the two, the Manetti is by far the better for this climate. It is very vigorous, very hardy, easily increased by layers or cuttings of the ripe wood, and free from the vicious habit of the Dog Rose, of throwing out long under-ground suckers. We would by no means say that it will not throw up an abundance of shoots from the roots if allowed to do so; but these shoots are easily distinguished by a practised eye from those of the budded rose. They may be known at a glance by the peculiar reddish tint of the stem, and by the shape and the deep glossy hue of the leaves.

They must be removed as soon as seen, not by cutting them off, but by tearing them off under ground, either by hand if possible, or with the help of a forked stick, which, pressed strongly into the earth, slips them off at their junction with the root.

It cannot be denied that many kinds of roses, budded low on the Manetti stock, will grow with a vigor, and bloom with a splendor, which they do not reach on their own roots, and which will often repay the additional labor which they exact. We once planted in the manner above described a strong Manetti stock containing a single bud of the Hybrid Perpetual Rose,—Triomphe de l'Exposition. In the September following, it had thrown up a stem with several branches, the central shoot rising to the height of six feet and a half, and bearing on its top the largest and finest blossom we have ever seen of that superb variety. Some roses, however, will not grow well on the Manetti. Others, again, can scarcely be grown with advantage in any other way, refusing to strike root from layers, and often failing when the attempt is made to root them from cuttings even of the soft wood. Some, even when rooted, remain feeble and dwarfish plants; while, if a bud from them is implanted in a good Manetti stock, it would grow to a vigorous bush in one season. To sum up, we would say, that, for the amateur, nine roses out of ten are better on their own roots, while there are a few which can only be grown successfully, budded on a good stock.

GRAFTING.

All the evil that can be spoken of budded roses is doubly true of grafted roses; while the advantages which the former can claim are possessed in a less degree by the latter. The reason is, simply, that, in the case of the budded rose, the junction between the stock and foreign variety is commonly more perfect than in the case of the grafted rose. Indeed, it would not be worth while to graft roses at all, were it not for the fact that grafting can be practised at times when budding is impossible. This is because it is indispensable, in budding, that the sap of the stock should be in full motion; whereas, in grafting, it may be at rest.

There are innumerable modes of grafting; but, for the rose, the simplest form of what is called "whip-grafting" is perhaps the best. In the end of winter, or at the beginning of spring, take young well-rooted plants of the Manetti stock, having stems not much larger than a quill. Beginning very near the root, shave off with a sharp knife a slip of the bark, with a little of the wood, to the length of something more than an inch; then shave down the lower end of the graft until it fits accurately the part of the stock whence the bark and wood have been pared off. The essential point is, that the inner bark of the graft should be in contact with the inner bark of the stock. When the two are fitted, bind them around with strings of wet bass-matting. Now plant the stock in a pot, setting it so deeply, that its point of junction with the graft is completely covered with soil. Place the pots thus prepared on a gentle hot-bed, and cover them closely with glass. When the shoots from the graft are well grown out, give them air by degrees to harden them.

A better way is to pot the stocks early in autumn, so that they may become well established. In this case, it will be necessary to cover the junction of the stock and graft with grafting wax or clay in such a manner as to exclude all air; then plunge the pots in old tan over a gentle hot-bed, so deeply that the grafted part is completely covered, the ends only of the grafts being visible. This keeps them in an equable heat and moisture. The subsequent treatment is the same as in the former case. As the stock has acquired a hold on the earth of the pot, or is, as the gardeners express it, "established," the graft will grow much more quickly, and make a strong blooming plant the same season.

In all grafting, whether of roses or other woody plants, it is necessary that the buds of the graft should be completely dormant. In the stock, on the other hand, a slight and partial awakening of the vital action at the time the graft is put on seems rather beneficial than injurious.

Suckers

In this mode of increasing roses, Nature, rather than the cultivator, may be said to do the work of propagation. Many sorts of roses throw out spontaneously long underground stems, from which roots soon issue, and which soon throw up an abundance of shoots above ground. When these suckers, as they are called, are separated from the parent, and planted apart, they make a strong growth, but rarely form plants so symmetrical as those raised from cuttings or layers.

MISCELLANEOUS OPERATIONS.

CHAP. IV.

RAISING NEW VARIETIES.—A layer, a cutting, a bud, a graft, and a sucker, are detached portions of an individual plant; and the plant resulting from them is of precisely the same character with the parent. But, when the seed germinates, it is not the reproduction of the same individual, but it is the birth of a new one. The offspring will show a family likeness; but it is by no means probable, at least in the case of the rose, that its features will be precisely the same with those of its parent. Plant the seeds of a rose; as, for example, of the Hybrid Perpetual, La Reine, and of the resulting seedlings: all will probably show traces, more or less, of their origin; but the greater part will be far inferior to the parent. Some will be single; many will be half double; and, among a large number of seedlings, we shall be fortunate if we find two or three equal in beauty to La Reine herself. Nor is it at all likely that even these will be her precise counterparts. They may possibly be her equals; but they will not exactly resemble her: and thus we obtain a new and valuable acquisition to the list of roses. Now, if, instead of singly gathering and sowing the seeds of La Reine, we first impregnate its flowers with the pollen of a different variety, such as the Giant of Battles, our chance of a valuable result is increased, because, if we are fortunate, we combine the desirable qualities of two sorts. It is not impossible that we may thus produce a rose combining the vigorous growth and large globular flowers of La Reine with some portion of the vivid coloring of the Giant of Battles. It is by the raising of seedlings with or without hybridization that the innumerable roses that decorate our gardens and fill the catalogues of nursery-men have been produced. M. Laffay, to whom more than to any other single cultivator we are indebted for bringing into existence the splendid family of the Hybrid Perpetual roses, raised in one year more than three hundred thousand seedlings. Of these, all but a small portion were, no doubt, pulled up, and thrown away as worthless, after their first blooming; the rest were allowed to stand for further trial: and if, finally, a score or two of roses really distinct and valuable were obtained, the year's culture may have been regarded as a great success. It requires a long time before the character of a seedling-rose can be thoroughly ascertained. M. Margottin, another eminent rose-grower, says that no conscientious cultivator will permit a seedling to pass out of his hands until he has given it a six-years' trial.

The raising of roses from seed is an occupation of so much interest, that few who have fairly entered upon it have ever willingly abandoned it. Many choice roses have been raised by amateurs; and those who have the time and means to enter on a large or a small scale upon this pursuit will find it a source of abundant enjoyment. In the next chapter, we shall point out the combinations from which the existing classes of Hybrid roses have sprung; and hereafter, when we come to the description of these classes, we shall add a few suggestions as to other combinations likely to produce good results.

Some roses bear seed freely, while others can hardly be induced to bear it at all. The hybridizer should take note of their peculiarities in this respect, or he will throw away much labor and patience; for it is a thankless task to hybridize a rose, which, after all the labor spent upon it, will not produce a single seed-vessel. Fortunately, many of the best roses bear seed abundantly; and La Reine, General Jacqueminot, Jules Margottin, Madame Laffay, and many others as good as these, may confidently be relied on. It is a good rule, that no seedling-rose is worth preserving, or at least worth propagating, that is not, in some one point, superior to or distinct from any other rose existing.

Roses should be hybridized immediately after they open, or they will become thoroughly fertilized with their own pollen, and the object of the operation will thus be defeated. The best time of the day is about ten o'clock in the morning, as soon as the sun has dried the dew from the centre of the flower. The pollen of the rose whose qualities it is wished to impart may be applied to the pistils of the maternal or seed-bearing flower with a camel's-hair pencil; or one rose may be held over the other, and tapped with the finger till the pollen falls upon the pistils of the seed-bearer. Roses are uncertain as to the production of pollen. In some seasons and some situations it is abundant, while in others it is produced very scantily. The impregnated roses may be marked by strings or labels tied to their stems. The seed should not be gathered till the first frost; and, to insure its ripening, the plant should stand in a warm, sunny exposure. The pods should be laid in the sun to dry, then broken up, and the seed separated by means of a sieve.

We have found the following mode of sowing a successful one: A frame — a shallow hot-bed frame answers perfectly — should be prepared by making within it a bed of loam, old manure, leaf-mould, and sand, at least eighteen inches deep. These materials should be thoroughly mixed, and the surface layer for an inch or two in depth sifted through a moderately coarse sieve, and then levelled and smoothed. The seeds may be sown broadcast; that is to say, scattered over the surface. They may be sown thickly, as not a third part will germinate; and, when sown, they should be pressed firmly into the soil with a board or the back of a spade. Then the same soil should be sifted over them to the depth of half an inch, and pressed down very lightly. Some will prefer to sow them in drills, which should be about six inches apart; the seed in no case being more than half an inch deep. Now leave the frame open, and exposed to rain and frost. Just before the heavy snows begin, and when the whole is hard frozen, cover it with boards and mats, that it may remain frozen till spring. The object of this is to protect the seeds from mice, which are exceedingly fond of them. When the mild weather begins, open the frame, and allow the ground to thaw: keeping, however, a close watch upon them; for, though these depredators like to do their work under cover and in darkness, there is still some little danger of their attacks. As the soil warms, the seeds will begin to come up. Some of the ever-blooming roses may blossom the first season; but the Hardy June kinds will not show bloom before the third, or even the fourth year. If the plants are too crowded, pull up some of them when the ground is softened after a rain, and plant them in a bed by themselves. In the autumn, take them all up, and heel them in a mouse-proof frame for safe keeping through the winter. In the spring, plant them out in rich soil, a foot apart. They might, indeed, be wintered safely in the frame where they originally grew: but this is attended with one disadvantage; for many of the seeds will not germinate till the second year; and, in removing the plants at that time, these infant seedlings would be destroyed; whereas, by leaving them undisturbed, a second crop may be obtained. Care must be taken throughout to keep the frame free from weeds.

The eminent English rose-grower, Mr. Rivers, recommends a method of raising seedlings, which we have not tried, but which we have no doubt is a good one, though not applicable to raising them on a large scale. We give his directions in his own words:—

"The hips of all the varieties of roses will, in general, be fully ripe by the beginning of November: they should then be gathered, and kept entire in a flower-pot filled with dry sand, carefully guarded from mice. In February, or by the first week in March, they must be broken to pieces with the fingers, and sown in flower-pots, such as are generally used for sowing seeds in, called 'seed-pans;' but, for rose-seeds, they should not be too shallow: nine inches in depth will be enough. . These should be nearly, but not quite, filled with a rich compost of rotten manure, and sandy loam or peat. The seeds may be covered to the depth of about half an inch with the same compost. A piece of kiln-wire must then be placed over the pot, fitting closely at the rim, so as to prevent the ingress of mice, which are passionately fond of rose-seeds. There must be space enough between the wire and the mould for the young plants to come up: half an inch will probably be found enough. The pots of seed must never be placed under glass, but kept constantly in the open air, in a full sunny exposure, as the wire will shade the mould, and prevent its drying. Water should be given occasionally in dry weather. The young plants will perhaps make their appearance in April or May; but very often the seed will not vegetate till the second spring. When they have made their 'rough leaves,' that is, when they have three or four leaves, exclusive of their seed-leaves, they must be carefully raised with the point of a narrow pruning-knife, potted into small pots, and placed in the shade: if the weather be very hot and dry, they may be covered with a hand-glass for a few days. They may remain in those pots a month, and then be planted out into a rich border: by the end of August, those that are robust growers will have made shoots long enough to take buds from. Those that have done so may be cut down, and one or two strong stocks budded with each: these will, the following summer, make vigorous shoots; and the summer following, if left unpruned, to a certainty they will produce flowers. This is the only method to insure seedling roses flowering the third year: many will do so that are not budded; but very often the superior varieties are shy bloomers on their own roots, till age and careful culture give them strength.

"It may be mentioned here, as treatment applicable to all seed-bearing roses, that, when it is desirable the qualities of a favorite rose should preponderate, the petals of the flower to be fertilized must be opened gently with the fingers.* A flower that will expand in the morning should

---

* "It requires some watchfulness to do this at the proper time: if too soon, the petals will be injured in forcing them open; and in hot weather, in July, if delayed only an hour or two, the anthers will be found to have shed their pollen. To ascertain precisely when the pollen is in a fit state for transmission, a few of the anthers should be gently pressed with the finger and thumb: if the yellow dust adheres to them, the operation may be performed. It requires close examination and some practice

be opened the afternoon or evening previous, and the anthers all removed with a pair of pointed scissors: the following morning, when this flower is fully expanded, it must be fertilized with a flower of some variety, of which it is desired to have seedlings partaking largely of its qualities. To exemplify this, we will suppose that a climbing Moss Rose with red or crimson flowers is wished for. The flowers of the Blush Ayrshire, which bears seed abundantly, may be selected, and, before expansion, the anthers removed. The following morning, or as soon after the operation as these flowers open, they should be fertilized with those of the Luxembourg Moss. If the operation succeed, seeds will be procured, from which the probability is that a climbing rose will be produced with the habit

---

to know when the flower to be operated upon is in a fit state to receive the pollen: as a general rule, the flowers ought to be in the same state of expansion; or, in other words, about the same age. It is only in cases where it is wished for the qualities of a particular rose to predominate that the removal of the anthers of the rose to be fertilized is necessary: thus, if a yellow climbing rose is desired by the union of the Yellow Brier with the Ayrshire, *every anther* should be removed from the latter, so that it is fertilized solely with the pollen of the former. In some cases, where it is desirable to have the qualities of both parents in an equal degree, the removal of the anthers need not take place: thus I have found by removing them from the Luxembourg Moss, and fertilizing that rose with a dark variety of Rosa Gallica, that the features of the Moss Rose are totally lost in its offspring, and they become nearly pure varieties of Rosa Gallica; but if the anthers of the Moss Rose are left untouched, and it is fertilized with Rosa Gallica, interesting hybrids are the result, more or less mossy. This seems to make superfetation very probable; yet Dr. Lindley, in 'Theory of Horticulture,' p. 332, 'thinks it is not very likely to occur.'"

and flowers of the Moss Rose, or at least an approximation to them; and as these hybrids often bear seed freely, by repeating the process with them, the at present apparent remote chance of getting a climbing Moss Rose may be brought very near.

"I mention the union of the Moss and Ayrshire roses by way of illustration, and merely to point out to the amateur how extensive and how interesting a field of operations is open in this way. I ought to give a fact that has occurred in my own experience, which will tell better with the sceptical than a thousand anticipations. About four years since, in a pan of seedling Moss roses was one with a most peculiar habit, even when very young: this has since proved a hybrid rose, partaking much more of the Scotch Rose than of any other, and, till the plant arrived at full growth, I thought it a Scotch rose, the seed of which had by accident been mixed with that of the Moss Rose, although I had taken extreme care. To my surprise, it has since proved a perfect hybrid, having the sepals and the fruit of the Provence Rose, with the spiny and dwarf habit of the Scotch Rose: it bears abundance of hips, which are all abortive.* The difference in the fruit of the Moss and Provence roses and that of the Scotch is very remarkable, and this it was which drew my particular attention

---

* "It is more than probable, that, if the flowers of this rose were fertilized with those of the single Moss Rose, they would produce seed from which some curious hybrid Moss roses might be expected."

to the plant in question. It was raised from the same seed and in the same seed-pan as the Single Crimson Moss Rose. As this strange hybrid came from a Moss Rose, accidentally fertilized, we may expect that art will do much more for us."

Improvement of Climbing Roses.

Some of the more hardy kinds of climbing roses, as, for example, the Queen of the Prairies, may be induced to wear borrowed robes, and assume beauties beyond those with which Nature endowed them. At the proper season, they may be budded here and there with some of the most hardy and vigorous of the June and Hybrid Perpetual roses. As these varieties bloom earlier than the Prairie roses, the period of bloom of the climber will be greatly protracted by this process, while at the same time it will be made to bear flowers incomparably finer in form and color than its own. It will be necessary, however, in our Northern climate, to protect it by nailing mats over it, since otherwise many of the buds will be winter-killed; and, as it is expected to yield more than its natural share of bloom, it should be stimulated with more than the usual manuring, and pruned more closely than the ordinary climbing roses.

Natural Standards.

We have before spoken of the difficulty of cultivating standard roses, or roses budded on tall stems, in our climate. It is possible, however, to produce a kind of standard without a resort to budding. We may choose some of the most hardy and vigorous of the June roses,— we may find such especially in the class known as the Hybrid Chinas,— and encourage the growth of a single, strong, upright stem, removing all other shoots from the base of the plant as fast as they appear. The stem should be kept straight by tying it to a stick till it has gained strength enough to hold itself erect. Thus, in a single season, we shall have, with some varieties, a stem five or six feet high. Early in spring, prune it down to the first healthy and plump bud. During the following season, allow no shoots to develop themselves, except at the top; and, in the succeeding spring, prune back these top-shoots to two or three eyes. All of these eyes will, in their turn, develop into shoots; and these, again, are to be pruned back like the first. Thus, in two or three seasons, we obtain a thick bushy head at the top of a tall upright stem; in short, a standard, capable of bearing even a New-England winter.

Effects of Frost on Soil.

It is always better to prepare beds for roses in the autumn, that they may have the benefit of a thorough exposure to the winter frost. With this view, the soil should be thrown up into ridges as roughly as possible. It will then be thoroughly frozen through, and subjected to all the changes of temperature during the season. This will not only tend to destroy worms and noxious insects, but it will separate the particles of the soil, and leave it light and pliable. Soil thrown into ridges can also be worked earlier in the spring than that which is left at its natural level.

The cardinal points of successful rose-culture are a good soil, good pruning, and good cultivation. By cultivation, we mean a repeated digging, hoeing, or forking of the earth around the plants, by which the surface is kept open, and enabled freely to receive the dew, rain, and air, with its fertilizing gases. Plants so treated will suffer far less in a drought than if the soil had been left undisturbed; for not only will it now absorb the dew at night, but it will freely permit the moisture which always exists at certain depths below the surface to rise, and benefit the thirsty roots. For a similar reason, the process of sub-soiling, or trenching, by which the earth is loosened and stirred to a great depth, is exceedingly beneficial to roses, since the lower portions of the disturbed soil are a magazine of moisture which the severest drought cannot exhaust.

With newly-planted roses it is well to practise "mulching" with manure; or, in other words, to place manure on the surface around the roots of the plants. This keeps the ground moist and open, while every rain washes down a portion of nutriment to the roots.

 GROUPING OF ROSES.

Roses may be planted in clumps, on the lawn, with far better effect than when arranged in formal beds. They may be separated according to their classes, as June roses, Bourbons, Hybrid Perpetuals, Mosses, &c.; and the effect will be vastly better, if, instead of mingling colors indiscriminately, each is placed by itself. Thus the pure white of Madame Plantier will form a rich contrast with the deep crimson of General Jacqueminot, the vivid rose of

Jules Margottin, the clear flesh-color of Ville de Bruxelles, and the pale rose of Baronne Prévost, each massed by itself; while all these varied hues are beautifully relieved by the fresh green of a well-kept lawn with its surrounding trees and shrubbery.

PART II.
DESCRIPTION OF THE ROSE

Chap. V. Groups & Families
" VI. Summer Roses.
" VII. Autumnal Roses.

GROUPS & FAMILIES.

CHAP. V.

LIKE ALL things living, in the world of mind or of matter, the rose is beautified, enlarged, and strengthened by a course of judicious and persevering culture, continued through successive generations. The art of horticulture is no leveller. Its triumphs are achieved by rigid systems of selection and rejection, founded always on the broad basis of intrinsic worth. The good cultivator propagates no plants but the best. He carefully chooses those marked out by conspicuous merit; protects them from the pollen of inferior sorts; intermarries them, perhaps, with other varieties of equal vigor and beauty; saves their seed, and raises from it another generation. From the new plants thus obtained he again chooses the best, and repeats with them the same process. Thus the rose and other plants are brought slowly to their perfect development. It is in vain to look for much improvement by merely cultivating one individual. Culture alone will not make a single rose double, or a dull rose brilliant. We cultivate the parent, and look for our reward in the offspring.

The village maiden has a beauty and a charm of her own; and so has her counterpart in the floral world,— the wild rose that grows by the roadside. Transplanted to the garden, and, with its offspring after it to the fourth and fifth generation, made an object of skilful culture, it reaches at last a wonderful development. The flowers which in the ancestress were single and small become double in the offspring, and expand their countless petals to the sun in all the majesty of the Queen of Flowers. The village maid has risen to regal state. She has lost her native virgin charm; but she sits throned and crowned in imperial beauty.

Now, all the roses of our gardens have some wild ancestress of the woods and meadows, from whom, in the process of successive generations, their beauties have been developed, sometimes by happy accidents, but oftener by design. Thus have arisen families of roses, each marked with traces of its parentage. These are the patricians of the floral commonwealth, gifted at once with fame, beauty, and rank.

The various wild roses differ greatly in their capacity of improvement and development. In some cases, the offspring grow rapidly, in color, fulness, and size, with every successive generation. In other cases, they will not improve at all; and the rose remains a wild rose still, good only for the roadside. With others yet, there seems to be a fixed limit, which is soon reached, and where improvement stops. It requires, even with the best, good culture and selection through several generations before the highest result appears. In horticulture, an element of stability is essential to progress. When the florist sees in any rose a quality which he wishes to develop and perfect, he does not look for success to the plant before him, but to the offspring which he produces from this plant. But this production and culture must be conducted wisely and skilfully, or the offspring will degenerate instead of improving.

There are different kinds of culture, with different effects. That which is founded in the laws of Nature, and aims at a universal development, produces for its result not only increased beauty, but increased symmetry, strength, and vitality. On the other hand, it is in the power of the skilful florist to develop or to repress whatever quality he may please. By artificial processes of culture, roses have been produced, beautiful in form and color, but so small, that the whole plant, it is said, might be covered with an egg-shell. These are results of the ingenious florists of China and Japan. The culture that refines without invigorating, belongs, it seems, to a partial or perverted civilization.

These several families of roses, resulting from the development of the several species of wild rose, have mingled together; in other words, they have intermarried: for Linnæus has shown that "the loves of the flowers" are more than a conceit of poetical fancy. From the fertilization of the flowers of a rose of one family with the pollen of a rose of another family arises a mixed offspring, called *hybrids*. Seeds — which are vegetable eggs — are first produced; and these seeds germinate, or hatch, into a brood of young plants, combining in some degree the qualities of their parents. As this process of intermixture may be carried on indefinitely, a vast number of new varieties has resulted from it.

The botanical classification of the rose is a perplexity to

botanists. Its garden classification — quite another matter — is no less a source of embarrassment to its amateur, not to say professional, cultivator. To many, indeed, its entire nomenclature is a labyrinth of confusion; and some have gone to the length of proposing to abolish distinctions, which, in their eyes, seem arbitrary or fanciful. These distinctions, however, are founded in Nature, though the superstructure built upon her is sometimes flimsy enough to justify the impatience of its assailants. The chief difficulty arises from the extent to which the hybridization of the rose has been carried, and the vast entanglement of combinations which has resulted. Out of a propensity to classify, where, in the nature of things, precise classification is impossible, has arisen the equivocal and shadowy character of many of the nominal distinctions.

Omitting less important divisions, the following are the groups into which cultivated roses are ordinarily divided: The Provence,* the Moss,* the French,* the Hybrid China, the Damask,* the Alba,* the Austrian Brier,* the Sweetbrier,* the Scotch,* the Double Yellow,* the Ayrshire,* the Sempervirens,* the Multiflora,* the Boursault,* the Banksia,* the Prairie.* These bloom once in the season. The following are perpetual or *remontant:* The China,* the Tea,* the Bourbon, the Hybrid Perpetual, the Perpetual Moss, the Damask Perpetual,* the Noisette, the Musk,* the Macartney,* the Microphylla.*

Some of the above are marked with a star*: these are roses of *pure blood.* The rest are roses of mixed or hybrid origin. By the former are meant those which have sprung, without intermixture, from the wild roses which grew naturally in various parts of the world, and which are the only roses of which the botanical classifier takes cognizance. Many of them are of great beauty, and would be highly prized for ornamental uses, were they not eclipsed by the more splendid double varieties, which the industry of the florist has developed from them. Each of these groups of unmixed roses, however modified in form, size, or color, retains, as already mentioned, distinctive features of the native type from which it sprang. Yet it often happens that the name is misapplied. Thus a rose called Damask is not always a Damask, but a hybrid between a Damask and some other variety. The true distinctive features of the group are thus rendered, in some nominal members of it, so faint, that they can scarcely be recognized. Leaving these bastards out of view, we will consider at present only the legitimate offspring of the various families of the rose.

On Mount Caucasus grows a single wild rose, from the seeds of which have sprung the numerous family of the Provence or Cabbage roses, very double, very large, and very fragrant. This race is remarkable for its tendency to *sport*, from which have resulted some of the most singular and beautiful forms of the rose. For example, a rose-colored variety of the Provence produced a branch bearing striped flowers, and from that branch has been propagated the Striped Provence. The Crested Moss is the product of another of these freaks, being of the pure Provence race. The Common Moss, and all its progeny, have the same origin; being derived, in all probability, from a sporting branch of one of the Provence roses.

The family of the French Rose, or Rosa Gallica, is of vast extent, and, though including many diverse shades of color, — some pale, some bright, others spotted, striped, or marbled, — is commonly recognized without much difficulty by its family features. It is a native of Southern Europe.

The wild progenitor of the Damask or Damascus roses is a native of Syria. The name *Damask*, by the way, is popularly applied to deep-colored roses in general; but its floral signification is very different. In this group, for the first time, we meet with a feature, which, desirable as it is, was not many years since regarded as rare and exceptional. June has always been regarded as the month of the rose; but some of the Damasks have the peculiarity of blooming twice, or more than twice, during the season. These have been placed in a group by themselves, and christened *Damask Perpetuals*. The *remontant* character, however, is not confined to them; for individual plants belonging to groups and varieties which usually bloom but once will sometimes display, an autumnal bloom. Thus the common wild rose of New England is now and then to be seen covered with flowers in September; and there is little doubt, that, from the seeds of these twice-blooming individuals, a new race of hardy *remontant* roses might be produced. It should be added, that many of the so-called Damask Perpetuals are not pure Damask, but crossed with the blood of other families.

Of the remaining races of pure blood, the Alba is remarkable for the delicate coloring of its flowers; the greater part being, as the name imports, white, or nearly so. The original variety grows wild in Central Europe.

The Austrian Brier is another family, of features very strongly marked. Yellow and copper are its prevailing colors; and from its habit of growth, and the color of its twigs, it is easily recognized under all its forms. Its original types are natives of the south of Europe, and probably of Persia; to which country we owe its finest development, — the well-known Persian Yellow.

The Double Yellow Rose, Rosa Sulphurea, remarkable for its beauty, and, in our climate, notorious for its intractable and uncertain character, is regarded by some botanists as belonging to a group distinct from the preceding. The Single Yellow, from which it must have sprung, has been found wild in the north of India.

The Sweet-brier, found wild in various parts of the world, is too well known to need further notice. The American variety differs distinctly from the European.

The Scotch roses owe their origin to the dwarf wild rose of Scotland. The Ayrshire is a family of climbing roses, originating from the wild trailing rose, Rosa Arvensis, common in the British islands. The best of them are said, however, to be hybrids between this rose and other species. The Boursault roses are descendants of Rosa Alpina, a native of the Alps; and no family is more clearly marked by distinctive features. The Sempervirens and the Multiflora are, with us at least, less familiar. Both are climbers, like the former; the one originating from a wild rose of Italy, the other from a wild rose of Japan. The Banksia, with its smooth, shining leaves, and slender, green stems, is well known in every greenhouse. Its progenitor is a native of China or Tartary, and the improved varieties are chiefly due to the labors of Chinese florists.

There is another race of climbers, held in great scorn by foreign florists, but admirably adapted to our climate, under whose influences they put forth beauties by no means contemptible. These are the progeny of the wild Michigan or Prairie Rose, rampant growers, and generally sturdy enough to outface our hardest winters. The best of them, however, the Baltimore Belle, is evidently the offspring of a foreign marriage, which, while contributing fragrance and beauty to the rugged race of the prairies, has detracted something from its hardihood. The union, probably accidental, seems to have been with the Tea Rose or the Noisette.

Of the foregoing groups, all except the Damask Perpetual are once-blooming. The following have, to a greater or less extent, the desirable character of a continued or successive bloom.

The Macartney Rose is a wild rose of China, from which a few improved varieties have been raised from seed. Its evergreen shining foliage is its most attractive feature. The Microphylla, or Small-leaved Rose, is closely akin to the Macartney, and, like the latter, is a native of the East.

The Musk is a rose much more familiarly known. It descends from a Persian or Syrian progenitor, and its vigorous growth, rich clusters of bloom, and peculiar fragrance, have long made it a favorite. But by far the most interesting and valuable among the unmixed races of ever-blooming roses are the numberless offspring of Rosa Indica, in its several varieties. To it we owe all the China and Tea-scented roses, while to its foreign alliances we are indebted for a vast and increasing host of brilliant hybrids.

Thus, from the families of pure blood, we come at length to those in which is mingled that of two or more distinct races. Convey the pollen of a China rose to the stigmas of a French, Damask, or Provence rose, and from the resulting seed an offspring arises different from either parent. Hence a new group of roses known as the Hybrid Chinas. The parents are both of moderate growth. The offspring is usually of such vigor as to form with readiness a pillar eight feet high. Its foliage is distinct, its bloom often as profuse and brilliant as that of the China, and its constitution as hardy, or nearly so, as that of the French Rose. Unlike the former, it blooms but once in the year, or only in a few exceptional instances shows a straggling autumnal flower. By a vicious system of subdivision, the group has been separated into Hybrid China, Hybrid Bourbon, and Hybrid Noisette. The two latter are the same as the first: except, in the one case, a slight infusion of the Damask Perpetual; and, in the latter, of the Musk Rose. In many cases, no human discernment could detect the effects of the admixture.

Again: convey the pollen of the China or Tea Rose to the flowers of the Musk, or *vice versâ;* and for a result we obtain the Noisette, inheriting from the former various striking characteristics of foliage and bloom, and from the latter its vigorous climbing habit and clustering inflorescence. But, by impregnation through several generations, some of the Noisettes retain so little of their Musk parent, that its traits are almost obliterated: they no longer bloom in clusters, and can scarcely be distinguished from the pure Tea Rose.

Again: a union of a Damask Perpetual with a China rose has produced a distinct race, of vigorous habit and peculiar foliage, possessing in a high degree the ever-blooming character of both its parents. It is hardier than the China Rose, though usually unable to bear a New-England winter unprotected. This is the Bourbon Rose, a brilliant and beautiful group, worth all the care which in this latitude its out-door culture requires.

The Moss Rose, impregnated with various ever-blooming varieties, has borne hybrids partially retaining the mossy stem and calyx, with a tendency more or less manifest to bloom in the autumn. Hence the group of the Perpetual Moss, a few only of whose members deserve the name.

It is evident, that, by continuing the process of hybridizing, hybrids may be mixed with hybrids, till the blood of half a score of the original races is mingled in one plant. This, in some cases, is, without doubt, actually the case; and this bastard progeny must, of necessity, be classified rather by its visible characteristics than by its parentage. Thus a host of ever-blooming hybrids, which are neither Noisette nor Bourbon nor Perpetual Moss, have been cast into one grand group, under the comprehensive title of Hybrid Perpetuals. Whence have they sprung? What has been their parentage? The question is easier asked than answered: for as, in a great nation of the West, one may discern the lineaments and hear the accents of diverse commingled races; so here we may trace the features of many and various families of Indian or Siberian, Chinese or European, extraction. The Hybrid Perpetuals, however, inherit their *remontant* character chiefly from Rosa Indica,—the China or Tea Rose,—and, in a far less degree, from the Damask Perpetual. An infusion of the former exists, in greater or less degree, in all of them; while the blood of the Damask Perpetual shows its traces in comparatively few. Many of the group are the results of a union between the Hybrid China roses and some variety of the China or Tea. Others owe their origin to the Hybrid China and the Bourbon, both parents being hybrids of Rosa Indica. Others are offspring of the Hybrid China crossed with the Damask Perpetual; while many spring from intermarriages within the group itself,— Hybrid Perpetual with Hybrid Perpetual.

By some over-zealous classifiers, this group has been cut up into various subdivisions, as Bourbon Perpetual, Rose de Rosomène, and the like; a procedure never sufficiently to be deprecated, as tending to produce no results but perplexity and confusion. Where there can be no definite basis of division, it is well to divide as little as may be; and it is to be hoped that secession from the heterogeneous commonwealth of the Hybrid Perpetuals will be effectually repressed. In regard to roses in general, while a classification founded on evident natural affinities is certainly desirable, yet, in the name of common sense, let us avoid the multiplication of new hybrid groups, founded on flimsy distinctions, and christened with new names, which begin with meaning little, and end with meaning nothing.

In our enumeration of the families and varieties of the rose, we shall make two great divisions, — that of the "Summer," or once-blooming, and that of the "Autumnal," or "ever-blooming" roses. In each of these divisions, we shall place first the roses of unmixed race, and, after them, the hybrids which have sprung from their combinations.

SUMMER ROSES
Chap. VI.

THESE ARE roses which bloom but once in the year; hence they have lost favor of late: for superb families of roses, fully equal in beauty, if not in hardiness, and endowed with an enviable power of renewing or perpetuating their charms, — of smiling in October as well as in June, and glowing in full effulgence even on the edge of winter, — have dazzled us into a forgetfulness of our ancient favorites.

Yet all the poetry of the rose belongs to these old roses of summer. It is they that bloomed in white and red in the rival shields of York and Lancaster; and it is they that, time out of mind, have been the silent interpreters of hearts too full to find a ruder utterance.

For the rest, they are, in the main, very hardy, very easy of culture, and often very beautiful.

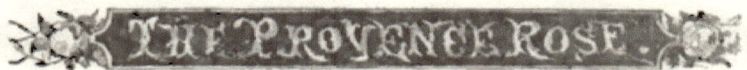

THE PROVENCE ROSE.

Rosa Centifolia.— This is the family of the old, well-known, and deservedly admired Cabbage Rose. Its ancestors, as we have seen, grew on Mount Caucasus; though some have supposed that it is a native of the south of France: hence the name Provence, by which it is often known in England, though it is never so designated in France. The French, translating its Latin name, Rosa Centifolia, or the Hundred-leaved Rose, commonly call it Rose à Cent Feuilles. It is supposed to have been known to the Romans, and to have been one of their favorite roses; and it was introduced into England before the end of the sixteenth century, where at least, until these latter days, it has been greatly admired and prized. Recently, however, the introduction of the families of hardy, ever-blooming roses, has thrown the Cabbage and all its compeers into the shade. Nevertheless, it is one of the most desirable of flowers; and even those who are disposed to pass it by with slight regard will never deny that some of the progeny which have arisen from it are unsurpassed in beauty and attractiveness. It is remarkable among roses for the singular changes, in horticultural language called "sports," which it has assumed, and which, among other results, have given rise to the entire family of Moss roses, of which we shall speak in the next section.

The prevailing colors in this group are light. The Cabbage Rose is a somewhat weak grower in a heavy soil, though in a light soil it grows vigorously. As a general rule, it needs close pruning. The members of the family are numerous; but, besides the Old Cabbage, the following are the best: The DUTCH PROVENCE is remarkable for the size of its flowers, in which respect it even surpasses the Old Cabbage. The UNIQUE PROVENCE is probably a sport from the Old Cabbage; that is to say, an accidental variation of the flowers on some particular branch; which branch being propagated, the accidental features become permanent. The Unique Provence, which is pure white, has, in its turn, produced another sport, called the STRIPED UNIQUE, the flowers being white, striped with lake; though they are very capricious in their coloring, sometimes opening pure white, and occasionally light rose. But a more remarkable sport of the Provence is the variety called the

CRESTED PROVENCE, ROSA CRISTATA, or, very commonly among us, the CRESTED MOSS. It is not, however, a true Moss, as its stems are smooth. Its peculiarity consists in a curious and very beautiful mossy growth about the calyx. This growth is developed in proportion to the vigor of the plant: therefore it should be strongly manured and closely pruned, as should the whole race of Provence roses. ADÉLINE, the DUC DE CHOISEUL, the STADTHOLDER, and, above all, the REINE DE PROVENCE, are beautiful varieties of this group. To it also belong a sub-group of Miniature or Pompone roses, well suited for edging beds. They bloom early, and are exceedingly pretty and graceful. Among the best of them are the WHITE BURGUNDY, the DWARF BURGUNDY, DE MEAUX, and SPONG.

The above are all old roses; for it is rarely that a cultivator of the present day will give himself the trouble to raise new varieties of any of the June roses, excepting always the Mosses, which can never be out of favor.

THE MOSS ROSE.

Rosa Centifolia Muscosa. — We have spoken of the tendency of the Provence Rose to "sport." The most widely known and the most beautiful of the results arising from this tendency is the Moss Rose and its varieties; for that such is the true origin of this unique family, there can be very little doubt. There is, however, no record of the first appearance of the Moss Rose. The original type of the race — the Old Red Moss — was introduced into England as early as 1596. It came immediately from Holland, but seems not to have originated there: indeed, to this day, we have remained in doubt as to whence it drew its birth. Of the large number of Moss roses now on the lists of nursery-men, some owe their origin to sporting branches, others to seed. Of the plants arising from the seed of a Moss rose, not more than one in three will show the characteristic of the parent; that is, the "moss:" the rest will be mere varieties of the Provence Rose. Sometimes a Moss rose will put forth a branch perfectly free from the mossy covering.

In cold, heavy soils, Moss roses are somewhat difficult of cultivation; but in a light, rich loam, and a sunny exposure, free from roots of growing trees, they thrive luxuriantly. They all require high enrichment. All excepting the strongest growers should be closely pruned; and, in the Northern States, it is well to give them protection in winter by means of pine-boughs, or by laying them down like raspberries.

Here, as in other classes of the rose, the hybridist has been at work. By impregnating Moss roses with the pollen of some of the ever-blooming sorts, a group of Perpetual Mosses has been produced. These have, to a greater or less extent, the ever-blooming quality; but this is acquired at some sacrifice of the peculiar beauty of the moss. They will receive a separate notice. Again: these roses have been fertilized with the pollen of the Hybrid China Rose; and the result is a Moss rose, remarkably vigorous in growth, and particularly well suited to form pillars. Any, however, of the more vigorous Mosses may be used for this purpose, provided always that they receive the highest culture in a warm and open exposure. We have it on the authority of the well-known English rose-grower, Mr. Paul, that, in the garden of an amateur near Cheshunt, there is a pillar of the Old Red Moss fifteen feet high!

At the present day, when the annual progeny of new Perpetual roses from the nurseries of France, with a humble re-enforcement from those of England, has eclipsed by numbers the old garden favorites, the well-remembered roses of our infancy, the Moss alone stands in tranquil defiance of this gay tide of innovation. Nothing can eclipse and nothing can rival her. She is, and ever will be, the favorite of poetry and art; and the eloquence of her opening buds, half wrapped in their mossy envelope, will remain through all generations a chosen interpreter of the language of youth and beauty.

ALICE LE ROY is a distinct and beautiful rose, very large, full, and mossy; color, lilac and rose; form, cupped: it grows vigorously. ANGÉLIQUE QUÉTIER is also of a rosy-lilac hue, large, very double, and very mossy: it grows freely, like the former. The BLUSH MOSS is of growth somewhat more moderate: the flower is large and full, the foliage fine, and stems and buds well mossed; color, clear pale pink. CELINA is of a deep, rosy crimson, sometimes verging to purple. The COMMON, or OLD MOSS, is still one of the most beautiful of the whole family. Its flowers are large and full, and of a pale rose-color and globular form. It is more abundantly mossed than most of its progeny; and none of them surpass it, indeed very few equal it, in the beauty of its half-opened bud. Its growth is tolerably vigorous, and foliage fine. LANEII is a vigorous and beautiful rose; flowers large, full, and globular; color, a light rosy-crimson. The buds are large, full, and well mossed; its growth is vigorous; and, under good cultivation, the whole plant, with its large and bright-green foliage, bears a striking appearance of thrift and health.

LUXEMBOURG is of a deep crimson, moderately double, and of growth nearly as vigorous as the last, with which the deep hue of its buds forms a striking contrast. MALVINA is a good rose, with clusters of pink flowers. ÉCLATANTE is of a deep pink, large, double, and well mossed. COMTESSE DE MURINAIS is one of the best of the White Mosses. Its flowers, though not so double as the Old Moss, are large, and of the purest white; and the growth is very vigorous. The CRIMSON or TINWELL MOSS somewhat belies its name; for its flowers are rather of a deep rose than crimson. It is, however, a beautiful variety. PRINCESS ADELAIDE is remarkable for the extreme vigor of its growth, and is evidently a hybrid of some of the Hybrid Bourbon or Hybrid China roses. It is admirably suited for a pillar or a wall, but requires a full sun, and, if closely pruned, will not bloom at all. It blooms in large clusters: the flowers are of a light glossy rose, very large and full; and, if not too closely pruned, they are very abundant. The WHITE BATH is an admirable White Moss, large and full in flower, and exquisite in bud. As it is of moderate growth, it will bear close pruning. PROLIFIC is a very beautiful variety, resembling the Old Moss. BARONNE DE WASSENAËR is a very vigorous rose, of a bright red, and flowering in clusters. CAPTAIN INGRAM is of a dark, velvety purple. GLOIRE DES MOUSSEUSES is very large and double, and of a blush-color. ROSA BONHEUR is of a bright rose-color. NUITS D'YOUNG is of a very dwarfed growth, and small deep-purple flowers. VANDAEL is purple, edged with lilac.

The above afford excellent examples of the various characteristics of the family of the Mosses. Additions in considerable number are still made to it every year; but it is very rarely that any decisive improvement upon the old varieties is shown in the recent seedlings.

"Moss roses, when grown on their own roots, require a light and rich soil: in such soils, they form fine masses of beauty in beds on lawns. The varieties best adapted to this purpose are the Common Moss, the Prolific, the Luxembourg, the Crimson, and Lane's Moss. Plants of these are procurable at a moderate price; and, by pegging down their shoots with hooked sticks, the surface of the bed will be covered with a mass of foliage and flowers. They require the same severe pruning as the Provence Rose. To have a succession of flowers on the same bed, half of the shoots may be shortened in March, the remainder the beginning of May, pruning closely as recommended for the Provence roses. By this method, the blooming season may be prolonged from a fortnight to three weeks. They should have an abundant annual dressing of manure on the surface in November, and the bed lightly stirred with the fork in February. . . .

"To raise Moss roses from seed is a most interesting employment for the genuine rose amateur; such a pleasing field is open, and so much may yet be done. The following directions will, I hope, assist those who have leisure, perseverance, and love for this charming flower. A plant of the Luxembourg Moss, or one of the Celina Moss, and one of the Single Crimson Moss, should be planted against a south wall, close to each other, so that their branches may be mingled. In bright, calm, sunny mornings, in June, about ten o'clock, those flowers that are expanded should be examined by pressing the fingers on the anthers. It will then be found if the pollen be abundant: if so, a flower of the former should be shaken over the latter; or, what perhaps is better, its flower-stalks should be fastened to the wall, so that the flower will be kept in an erect position. Then cut a flower of the Luxembourg Moss, strip off its petals with a sharp pair of scissors, and place the anthers firmly, but gently, upon a flower of the Single Crimson, so that the anthers of each are entangled: they will keep it in its position: a stiff breeze will then scarcely remove it. The fertilizing will take place without further trouble, and a fine hip full of seed will be the result. To obtain seed from the Luxembourg Moss, I need scarcely say that this operation must be reversed. A wall is not always necessary to ripen seed; for in dry soils, and airy, exposed situations, the above Moss roses bear seed in tolerable abundance. The treatment of the hips, sowing the seed, and the management of the young plants, as applicable to all, has already been given." — *Rivers.*

THE DAMASK ROSE.

Rosa Damascena. — Any deeply colored rose is popularly called a Damask; but the true Damask — the rose of Damascus — is of various shades, from the darkest to the lightest. All these varieties have sprung from one origin, — the wild rose of Syria, which was introduced into England in the year 1573, or, according to some writers, much earlier. It is this rose from which is made the rose-water of the East, and on this the Eastern poets and their Western imitators have lavished the wealth of their fancy. In poetry, indeed, the Damask Rose has woven more garlands than the Moss. Nor is it unknown to history, since the five hundred camel-loads of rose-water with which the Sultan Saladin purified the Mosque of Omar after it had been used as a Christian church were doubtless distilled from its leaves. But, without falling into an anachronism, it is hardly possible to claim for it, as some have done, the honor of having been the renowned Red Rose of Lancaster.

Both the Damask and the Provence roses are extensively cultivated in France and England for the purpose of making rose-water.

The Damask is very hardy, vigorous of growth, and abundant in bloom. Its shoots are full of spines, and its leaves of a light green. Its old original varieties are wholly eclipsed by those which the industry of the florist has produced from their seed. The following are among the best of these:—

LA VILLE DE BRUXELLES is a very beautiful rose, of delicate waxy tint and vigorous growth. MADAME STOLTZ is of a pale straw or lemon color. MADAME SOËTMANS is of delicate cream-color, tinged with buff. MADAME HARDY is a large and very full rose of the purest white. It has but one fault,—that of sometimes showing a green bud in the centre. But for this, it would be almost unrivalled among white roses. LEDA is of a blush tint, edged with lake.

There are but few new varieties of this family, as the double sorts do not bear seed freely.

THE ALBA ROSE.

Rosa Alba.—The parent of the Alba, or White roses, is a native of Central Europe. The species is so called from the prevailing delicacy of hue in its varieties, many of which are of a pure white, while none are of a deeper coloring than a bright pink. The original stock is spineless; but many of its progeny, in consequence, probably, of hybridization, have spines in greater or less number. The upper surface of the leaves has a glaucous or whitish tinge, and the shoots are of a clear green.

FÉLICITÉ is a large double rose, of a delicate flesh-color, and a most symmetrical shape. LA SÉDUISANTE is of a bright rose in the centre, shading into flesh-color at the circumference: it rivals the last in the perfection of its shape. MADAME AUDOT is of a pale flesh-color. MADAME LEGRAS is a white rose of a peculiar delicacy, and very graceful in its habit of growth. THE QUEEN OF DENMARK is of a clear rosy pink. SOPHIE DE MARSILLY is of a delicate rose-color, slightly mottled, and, when half opened, is a rose of remarkable beauty.

The Alba roses bloom abundantly, and form in masses a beautiful contrast, in their chaste and delicate hues, with the deeper colors of the French and Hybrid China roses. They rarely bear seed freely.

THE FRENCH ROSE.

Rosa Gallica.—This rose draws its origin from the south of Europe, where its wild progenitor still grows abundantly in the hedges. It is one of the best known, and longest under cultivation, of all the species. We confess our strong partiality for it. It is perfectly hardy, compact in growth, abundant in bloom, beautiful in form, and rich and various in coloring. It will grow and bloom anywhere, and endures neglect with a patience unknown to most others of its race. Yet none better rewards a careful and generous culture. It returns a rich response to the care bestowed upon it; and, under high cultivation, the members of this group have no superiors in beauty. It is not, however, in favor at the present day. Roses of equal beauty, though not of equal hardihood, and endowed with the one valuable quality in which it is wanting,— that of continuous or repeated blooming,—have, of late, supplanted it. We may as well say here, while protesting against the neglect into which the hardy June roses have fallen, that, of the so-called Perpetuals, a great many are undeserving of the name. Some, even with tolerably good treatment, rarely show a flower after the June blooming; and none will put forth freely and abundantly in autumn, without more pains in the management than most persons are willing to bestow.

The French Rose has been known in England since the close of the sixteenth century. It is very prolific, and innumerable seedlings have been raised from it. Some of these produce flowers exceedingly double, of the most vivid color, and remarkable even now for the symmetry of their forms. Among the rest is a great variety of marbled, striped, and spotted roses, which, though curious and interesting, are certainly less beautiful than the "self-colored" sorts.

The varieties of this rose formerly catalogued and cultivated might be numbered by hundreds. Of these, it is needless to mention any but a few of the best and most distinct.

BOULA DE NANTEUIL is a rose of the richest crimson-purple, with a centre, at times, of a vivid red. It varies, however, very much in different seasons, and, while sometimes splendid in coloring, is occasionally dull and cloudy. GRANDISSIMA is of a deep purplish-rose, very large and double. KEAN closely resembles it. ADÈLE PRÉVOST is of a silvery blush. BLANCHEFLEUR is white, with a tinge of flesh-color. CYNTHIA is of a pale rose. THE DUCHESS OF BUCCLEUGH is of a dark rose. OHL is of a deep crimson and scarlet, and, when grown in perfection, is one of the finest roses in existence. LA REINE DES FRANÇAIS is also of a bright crimson. PERLE DES PANACHÉES is white, striped with rose; and ŒILLET PARFAIT is white, striped with light crimson, much like a carnation. D'AGUESSEAU, GLOIRE DE COLMAR, LATOUR D'AUVERGNE, TRIOMPHE DE JAUSSENS, LETITIA, NAPOLÉON, DUC DE VALMY, and TRANSON GOUBAULT, are all excellent roses of this family.

"To grow them fine for exhibition, as single blooms or 'show-roses,' the clusters of buds should be thinned early in June, taking at least two-thirds of the incipient flowers from each: manure should also be laid round their stems on the surface, and manure-water given to them plentifully in dry weather. With this description of culture, these roses will much surpass any thing we have yet seen in this country.

"Although the varieties of this group are summer roses only, their period of flowering may be prolonged by judicious pruning; and for this purpose two trees of each variety should be planted, one to be pruned in October, the other early in May, or just when the buds have burst into leaf: these will give a regular succession of flowers. In pruning, cut out with a sharp knife all the spray-like shoots, and then shorten to within six or eight buds of their base all the strong shoots (by such I mean those that are above fifteen inches in length): the weak shoots cut down to two or three buds. This is the pruning required by the Alba, Damask, and Hybrid Provence roses. . . .

"To raise French roses from seed, they should be planted in a warm, dry border sloping to the south, in an open, airy situation: the shade of trees is very pernicious to seed-bearing roses. The following kinds * may be selected, as they bear seed freely: The Tuscany Rose, a very old variety, with rich, deep crimson, semi-double flowers; also Ohl and Latour d'Auvergne. The two latter should have their flowers fertilized with the pollen of the Tuscany Rose, and some fine crimson roses will probably be raised. The Village Maid and Œillet Parfait are the most eligible to raise striped roses from: if their flowers are deficient in pollen, they should be fertilized with those of Rosa Mundi." — *Rivers.*

The Hybrid Chinese Rose.

Rosa Indica Hybrida. — This class has been divided by some writers into three; viz., Hybrid China, Hybrid

---

* Some of the roses recommended for seed-bearing are old varieties, which may be procured from any old-fashioned English rose-nursery.

Noisette, and Hybrid Bourbon. The division seems to us needless, for the reason that all these, on analysis, resolve themselves into hybrids of the Chinese Rose, since both the Noisette and the Bourbon owe their distinctive character to their Chinese parentage. The hybrids of the Noisettes are usually inclined to bloom in clusters: those of the Bourbons are distinguishable by their large, smooth, and thick leaves.

This class, then, may be defined as the offspring of intermarriage of the French and other June roses with the Chinese Rose and its hybrids. It has, however, none of the ever-blooming qualities which distinguish the China roses. It is remarkable, as a class, for vigor of growth, in which, strange as it may appear, it surpasses, in some cases, both its parents. Most of the Hybrid China roses are, moreover, perfectly hardy even in the climate of the Northern States; and they are admirably adapted for forming pillars. For this purpose, they should be planted in a very deep and rich soil. If the soil is naturally poor, dig it out to the width and depth of three feet, and replace it with a mixture of strong loam and old manure. Some of the Hybrid Chinas thus generously treated, and trained and pruned in the manner recommended in a former chapter, will form most gorgeous decorations of a garden; for in the size of the flowers, in beauty of form, and brilliancy of color, some of the varieties are unsurpassed. Every autumn, the surface of the soil around the stem should be covered with manure to the depth of several inches; and this should be allowed to remain throughout the summer, renewing it as often as necessary, after a previous forking-up of the soil, which this covering or "mulching" enriches, at the same time that it keeps it moist and cool.

The following are among the best of this family of roses: BEAUTY OF BILLIARD, of vigorous growth, and bright-scarlet and crimson flowers. BRENNUS, or BRUTUS, is a superb rose, of great size, and strong, rapid growth. BLAIRII, No. 2, is particularly adapted for a pillar rose; its bloom being very profuse. The color of its flowers is pink or blush. GEORGE THE FOURTH is an old rose raised some forty years ago by the excellent English cultivator, Mr. Rivers. Its bright crimson color and its neat foliage make it very attractive, though it is less double than some other varieties. THE DUKE OF DEVONSHIRE is of a lilac-color, striped with white, and perfect in form; its petals overlapping with the greatest regularity. CHARLES DUVAL is of a deep pink; CHARLES LAWSON, of a vivid rose. CHÊNEDOLÉ is regarded by many as the best rose of the class; for its color is the brightest and clearest crimson, and its flowers are large and very full. Inferior roses, however, are frequently sold under its name, especially in this country. COUPE D'HÉBÉ is remarkable both for the perfection of its cup-like form, and for the delicate rose-color of its petals. Its growth is very vigorous; and, like most of its kindred, it is perfectly hardy. GENERAL JACQUEMINOT is a large purplish-crimson rose. It must not be confounded with the Hybrid Perpetual of the same name. FULGENS is of a deep crimson. TRIOMPHE DE BAYEUX is white, and an excellent pillar-rose. MADAME PLANTIER is also white, but very distinct from the last; for, as it sprang on the mother's side from the Noisette, it blooms in clusters. Its individual flowers are surpassed by those of one or two other white roses; but the extraordinary profusion of its bloom, its graceful habit, its neat foliage, and its hardy, enduring nature, make it, on the whole, the best rose of its color in cultivation. PAUL PERRAS is Bourbon on the mother's side, as is also PAUL RICAUT. The first is of a pale rose, the second of a bright crimson. VIVID is a seedling of the English rose-grower, Mr. William Paul. Its flowers are not large, but they are of the most vivid crimson; and the vigorous habit of the plant makes it very suitable either for a pillar or a trellis.

"When grown as large standards, these roses require peculiar pruning. If their shoots are shortened too much, they will grow vigorously, but give no flowers. They should, therefore, be thinned out, so that the head of the tree is not at all crowded, and then be shortened to within twelve buds of their base: a crop of fine flowers will then be produced. This is the pruning to be done either in the early part of November or in February: we will call it the winter pruning.* There is another mode of pruning these roses, partly in summer, which will be found highly eligible. Thin out the shoots in the winter, and leave a selected number of those that are most vigorous nearly their full length, merely cutting off their tips: these will be loaded with blossoms so as to make the trees quite pendulous. As soon as the blooming season is past, shorten them all to within six inches of their base. They will immediately put forth strong shoots, which, while in a very young state, thin out, leaving those that are the most vigorous. These shoots treat in the same manner the following year. By this method of pruning, a pendulous, graceful head is formed, instead of a stiff, formal one, so common to standard roses. In pruning these roses, when trained as pillars, the spurs from the shoots fastened to the stake merely

---

* These directions, it will be remembered, are for the climate of England. The November pruning will not do here; indeed, it will require much precaution to make even the hardy roses succeed as standards.

require thinning out, so as not to be crowded, and then shortened to within five or six buds of their base. Trained as pillar-roses, they give flowers often too abundantly; so that they are small and ill-shaped: it is, therefore, often a good practice to thin the flower-buds as soon as they can be distinguished.

"I shall now proceed to give a list of those roses, from which, in combination with others, choice seedlings may be raised.

"The Duke of Devonshire, in a very warm and dry soil, will produce hips in tolerable abundance; and, as it is inclined to be striped, it would possibly form a beautiful combination with some striped rose, which should be planted with it.

"Riego, which partakes of the Sweet-brier, might be made the parent of some beautiful brier-like roses by planting it with the Splendid Sweet-brier.

"General Allard, a hybrid rose, from which Monsieur Laffay raised his perpetual rose, Madame Laffay, is much inclined to give a second series of flowers. This rose should be planted in a very warm border, or trained against a south wall with Bourbon Gloire de Rosomènes; and, if carefully fertilized with it, some beautiful crimson autumnal roses would probably be originated. Chênedolé may also be subjected to the same treatment. What a fine autumnal rose one like it would be!"— *Rivers.*

The Scotch Rose.

Rosa Spinosissima.—The original Scotch Rose is a wild dwarf rose, common in Scotland and the north of England. As it bears seed in great abundance, as these seeds vegetate freely, and as the Scotch gardeners have taken pride in multiplying and improving this native growth of the soil, the number of varieties is nominally immense. Many of them, however, are scarcely to be distinguished the one from the other. The flowers are small, and exceedingly numerous. They bloom earlier than most roses, and show various shades of crimson, rose, white, and yellow, or rather straw-color; for the yellow Scotch Rose is apparently a hybrid. They are useful for covering banks and forming clumps where masses of bloom are required. Nothing can exceed their hardiness, and they increase abundantly by suckers. A list of named varieties of the Scotch Rose would, from their multiplicity, and want of distinctness, be even more unsatisfactory than the florist's lists of pansies or verbenas. The following, however, are good:—

LA NEIGE is pure white, and very double. GUY MANNERING is of a deep blush. SULPHUREA, LADY BAILLIE, and the MARCHIONESS OF LANSDOWNE, are of a pale straw or sulphur color. The YELLOW SCOTCH is of a deeper yellow tint. FLORA, DAPHNE, EREBUS, VENUS, and the COUNTESS OF GLASGOW, are of deep shades of rose and crimson.

"Scotch roses, when grown into beds and clumps as dwarfs, are beautiful; and in early seasons they will bloom nearly a fortnight before the other summer roses make their appearance. This, of course, makes them desirable appendages to the flower-garden. They bear seed profusely; and raising new varieties from seed will be found a most interesting employment. To do this, all that is required is to sow the seed as soon as ripe, in October, in pots or beds of fine earth, covering it with nearly an inch of mould: the succeeding spring they will come up, and bloom in perfection the season following.

"The aim should be to obtain varieties with large and very double crimson flowers: this can only be done by slightly hybridizing; and to effect this it will be necessary to have a plant or two of the Tuscany Rose trained to a south wall, so that their flowers are expanded at the same time as the Scotch roses in the open borders: unless thus forced, they will be too late. Any dark-red varieties of the Scotch roses, such as Venus, Erebus, or Flora, should be planted separately from others, and their flowers fertilized with the above French Rose. Some very original deep-colored varieties will probably be obtained by this method. Sulphurea and one or two other straw-colored varieties may be planted with the Double Yellow Austrian Brier; and most likely some pretty sulphur-colored roses will be the result of this combination." — *Rivers.*

Rosa Lutea. — This is a small family of roses, very distinct in all its characteristics; a native of Southern Europe and of some parts of the East. It is seldom that any seedlings have been obtained from it, as its flowers, even in the single varieties, are usually barren. They may, however, be made productive by fertilizing them with the pollen of other varieties. Its stems are spiny, and of a reddish or brownish color. Its leaves are small, and its growth somewhat straggling. The colors of its flowers are copper and yellow in various shades. It should not be pruned too closely; but the shoots may with great advantage be pinched back in midsummer, thus causing them to throw out a great number of lateral shoots, and correcting the loose and straggling habit of the bush. The bloom, with this treatment, is very profuse.

The best known roses of this family are five in number. The SINGLE AUSTRIAN YELLOW and the SINGLE AUSTRIAN COPPER may be regarded as the original types of the species. WILLIAM'S DOUBLE YELLOW is an English seedling of a pale-yellow color. HARRISON'S YELLOW is an excellent yellow rose, originated in America. It is very vigorous in growth, and, on the whole, the best yellow rose for general cultivation. The PERSIAN YELLOW, however, is of a much deeper hue, and is unrivalled in its way. It is one of those roses which are feeble on their own roots, but grow very vigorously either on the Dog Rose or on the Manetti stock. It is said to have originated, as its name imports, from Persia.

A moist soil, and a dry, pure air, are essential to the growth of all this family of roses.

"No family of roses offers such an interesting field for experiments in raising new varieties from seed as this. First we have the Copper Austrian, from which, although it is one of the oldest roses in our gardens, a double flowering variety has never yet been obtained. This rose is always defective in pollen; and consequently it will not bear seed unless its flowers are fertilized. As it will be interesting to retain the traits of the species, it should be planted with and fertilized by the Double Yellow: it will then, in warm, dry seasons, produce seed, not abundantly;

but the amateur must rest satisfied if he can procure even one hip-full of perfect seed.

"The beautiful and brilliant Rosa Harrisonii, however, gives the brightest hopes. This should be planted with the Double Yellow Brier: it will then bear seed abundantly. No rose will, perhaps, show the effects of fertilizing its flowers more plainly than this; and consequently, to the amateur, it is the pleasing triumph of Art over Nature. Every flower on my experimental plants, not fertilized, proved abortive; while, on the contrary, all those that were so, produced large black spherical hips-full of perfect seed. The Persian Yellow does not seem inclined to bear seed; but it may be crossed with Rosa Harrisonii, and, I trust, with some good effect." — *Rivers.*

THE DOUBLE YELLOW ROSE.

Rosa Sulphurea. — This beautiful rose is difficult of cultivation both in England and in this country, though in Italy and the south of France it grows and blooms luxuriantly. Its original species is found growing wild, and yielding single flowers, on the Himalaya Mountains, and also, it is said, in Persia. Only two varieties are in cultivation, — the DOUBLE (called also the YELLOW PROVENCE) and the DWARF DOUBLE. The climate of the

Southern and Middle States is far more suitable to them than that of the North; though it is more than probable, that, with careful and judicious treatment, they would do well even here. They need a rich diet, and a sunny and airy situation, to induce them to expand their flower-buds, which are provokingly apt to fall before opening. They are also very liable to the attacks of insects. The difficulty of the cultivation of this rose is greatly to be lamented, since it surpasses even the Persian Yellow in beauty.

"Various situations," says Mr. Rivers, "have been recommended. Some have said, 'Plant it against a south wall;' others, 'Give it a northern aspect, under the drip of some water-trough, as it requires a wet situation.' All this is quackery and nonsense. The Yellow Provence Rose is a native of a warm climate, and therefore requires a warm situation, a free and airy exposure, and rich soil: a wall with a south-east or north-west aspect will be found eligible. Give the plants surface-manure every autumn, and water with manure-water in May; prune with the finger and thumb in summer, as recommended for the Persian Yellow.*

"At Burleigh, the seat of the Marquis of Exeter, the effect of situation on this rose is forcibly shown. A very

---

* M. Godefroy, a French nursery-man, has cultivated it as a pillar-rose, in a free and open situation, with much success. Manuring as above, and summer pruning, are indispensable.

old plant is growing against the southern wall of the mansion, in a confined situation, its roots cramped by a stone pavement: it is weakly, and never shows a flower-bud. In the entrance-court is another plant, growing in front of a low parapet wall, in a good loamy soil, and free, airy exposure: this is in a state of the greatest luxuriance, and blooms in fine perfection nearly every season.

"Mr. Mackintosh, the gardener, who kindly pointed out these plants to me, thought the latter a distinct and superior variety, as it was brought from France by a French cook a few years since; but it is certainly nothing but the genuine Old Double Yellow Rose.

"In unfavorable soils, it will often flourish and bloom freely if budded on the Musk Rose, the common China Rose, or some free-growing hybrid China Rose; but the following pretty method of culture I beg to suggest: Bud or graft it on some short stems of the Rosa Manetti. In the autumn, pot some of the strongest plants; and, late in spring, force them with a gentle heat, giving plenty of air. It will now also be very interesting to plant trees of this variety in orchard-houses: this seems to me to be the exact climate required by it. By this method, the dry and warm climate of Florence and Genoa may, perhaps, be partially imitated; for there it blooms in such profusion, that large quantities of its magnificent flowers are daily sold in the markets during the rose-season.

"The following extract relative to this rose is from the

quaint old book, 'Flora, Ceres, and Pomona, by John Rea, Gent., 1655,' showing that budding and double-budding of roses and trees is no new idea: 'The Double Yellow Rose is the most unapt of all others to bear kindly and fair flowers, unless it be ordered and looked unto in an especial manner. For whereas all other roses are best natural, this is best inoculated upon another stock. Others thrive and bear best in the sun, this in the shade. Therefore the best way that I know to cause this rose to bring forth fair and kindly flowers is performed after this manner: First, in the stock of a Francford * Rose, near the ground, put in a bud of the Single Yellow Rose, which will quickly shoot to a good length; then, half a yard higher than the place where the same was budded, put into it a bud of the Double Yellow Rose; which growing, the suckers must be kept from the root, and all the buds rubbed off, except those of the kind desired; which being grown big enough to bear (which will be in the two years), it must in winter be pruned very near, cutting off all the small shoots, and only leaving the biggest, cutting off the tops of them also, as far as they are small; then in the spring, when the buds for leaves come forth, rub off the smallest of them, leaving only some few of the biggest, which by reason of the strength of the stock affording more nourishment than any other, and the agreeable nature of the Single Yellow Rose

---

* This is the Frankfort Rose, a variety of Rosa Gallica, with very double flowers, one of our oldest garden-roses.

(from whence it is immediately nourished), the shoots will be then strong, and able to bear out the flowers if they be not too many, which may be prevented by nipping off the smallest buds for flowers, leaving only such a number of the fairest as the tree may be able to bring to perfection; which tree should stand something shadowed, and not too much in the heat of the sun, and in a standard by itself, rather than under a wall. These rules being observed, we may expect to enjoy the full delight of these beautiful roses, as I myself have often done by my own practice in divers trees so handled, which have yearly borne store of fair flowers, when those that were natural, notwithstanding all the helps I could use, have not brought forth one that was kindly, but all of them either broken, or, as it were, blasted.'"

Rosa Rubignosa.— This is the Eglantine of the poets, celebrated in song by bards known and unknown to fame, from Milton down to the rustic rhymer offering the tribute of his untutored Muse to the charms of some village beauty.

Nothing is easier than its cultivation; but, to our mind, it loses half its attraction when transplanted from its native road-side or thicket into the garden. From its perfect hardiness and free growth, it is sometimes used as a stock for budding or grafting. The fragrance of its leaves readily distinguishes it from other species.

Most of the named varieties under this head in the catalogues of nursery-men are hybrids; sometimes, as in the case of the DOUBLE-MARGINED HIP, or MADELINE, retaining little trace of the SWEET-BRIER. Among the best are the MONSTROUS SWEET-BRIER, the CARMINE, the CELESTIAL, the SPLENDID, the SCARLET, the ROSE ANGLE, the ROYAL, and the SUPERB.

Rosa Alpina.— This familiar climbing rose is easily known by its long shoots, nearly or quite free from thorns, and the reddish tinge, shaded into green, which marks the stems of most of the varieties. Its parent is a native of the Alps, and it is perfectly hardy. The flowers grow in clusters. In the OLD RED BOURSAULT, they are semi-double, and indifferently formed; but some of the other varieties show great improvements both in shape and color. They are excellent climbing or pillar roses, and require less sun to develop their flowers than most other species. Like other climbing roses, they should be pruned but little, though the old stems should be well thinned out.

AMADIS, or the CRIMSON BOURSAULT, is of a deep purplish-crimson, with large semi-double flowers. The BLUSH BOURSAULT is, in its flowers, larger and more full than most others of the species. They are of a deep flesh-color, passing into a lighter shade towards the edge. It can scarcely owe its qualities to the Boursault race alone, but seems to be a hybrid of some of the Chinese roses. When in perfection, it is much the best of the group, but requires a warmer and brighter aspect than the others. It is, however, perfectly hardy. This variety is also called CALYPSO, DE L'ISLE, The WHITE BOURSAULT, and FLORIDA. INERMIS ELEGANS and GRACILIS are the only other varieties of the group that need be mentioned here.

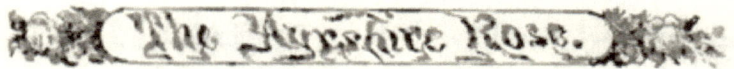

The Ayrshire Rose.

Rosa Arvensis Hybrida.—The origin of the Ayrshire Rose has been the subject of some discussion among botanists and cultivators. It is generally supposed, however, to have sprung from the seed of a wild trailing rose common in Great Britain and in Western Europe, the flowers of which had been impregnated by accident or design with the pollen of some other species. The Ayrshire roses are known in Europe for their astonishing vigor of growth; some species, it is said, growing nearly thirty feet in a year, — an achievement which we never knew them to equal in this country. Their growth, however, is very rapid; and, when once established, their long, slender shoots quickly possess themselves of every object near them. As may be gathered from their name, most of them originated in Scotland. In Europe, these roses are valued as standard weepers, since, when budded on tall stocks, they form huge heads of pendulous foliage and bloom. Doubtless they would succeed as well or better in our Southern and Middle States; but in the North they would probably require, in common with other standard roses, a careful protection against the changes of the seasons.

BENNETT'S SEEDLING and the DUNDEE RAMBLER have white flowers; those of the last being not fully double. The COUNTESS OF LIEVEN is creamy-white and semi-double. SPLENDENS is white, edged with red; and the QUEEN OF THE BELGIANS is of a cream-color. The AYRSHIRE QUEEN is of a dark crimson-purple, and less vigorous in growth than the rest. RUGA is of a pale flesh-color. Like the last, it is a hybrid, probably between the

Tea Rose and one of the Ayrshires; for it has much of the fragrance of the former.

"I have a steep bank of a hard white clay," says an English writer, "which, owing to a cutting made in the road, became too steep for cultivation. About sixteen years since, this was planted with Ayrshire and other climbing roses. Holes were made in the hard soil with a pick, two feet over and two feet deep; some manure mixed with the clay, after it had lain exposed to frost to mellow it, and climbing roses planted. This bank is, when the roses are in bloom, a mass of beauty: I have never seen any thing in climbing roses to equal it. On another bank, they are gradually mounting to the tops of the trees: none of them have ever been pruned. Ayrshire roses, as articles of decoration in places unfitted for other ornamental climbers, are worthy of much more attention than they have hitherto received.

The following extract from the "Dundee Courier" of July 11, 1837, will give some idea how capable these roses are of making even a wilderness a scene of beauty:—

"Some years ago, a sand-pit at Ellangowan was filled up with rubbish found in digging a well. Over this a piece of rock was formed for the growth of plants which prefer such situations, and amongst them were planted some half-dozen plants of the Double Ayrshire Rose, raised in this neighborhood about ten years ago. These roses now most completely cover the whole ground,— a space of thirty feet by twenty. At present they are in full bloom, showing probably not less than ten thousand roses in this small space."

THE EVERGREEN ROSE.

Rosa Sempervirens.— This is a climbing rose of very vigorous growth, a native of the middle and south of Europe. The garden varieties originated from it bloom in clusters of small and usually very double flowers, of which the prevailing tints are light, varying from delicate shades of rose and pink to a pure white. They are not absolutely evergreen, but only partially so, retaining their bright, glossy leaves till spring, provided they are planted in shady and sheltered places, as under trees, or in the angles of walls, but dropping them in open situations. In England they have come into great favor as pillar-roses, and for covering walls, banks, or unsightly objects in the garden or on the pleasure-ground. Budded on tall stems of the Dog Rose, they form pendulous standards of magnificent proportions; rivalling, in this respect, the Ayrshire. Whether such standards would be equally successful in the Northern States, is, to say the least, doubtful.

Most of the varieties of the Evergreen Rose now most in esteem were originated in the gardens of Neuilly, near Paris, by M. Jacques, gardener to King Louis Philippe. One or two are crossed with the Musk Rose; whence they acquire a fragrance in which their own race is deficient. BANKSLEFLORA is one of these. It has small double white flowers. FÉLICITÉ PERPÉTUÉE, in spite of its preposterous name, is one of the most beautiful of climbing roses; and trained as it sometimes is in European gardens, drooping in graceful festoons from pillar to pillar on supporting wires, or mantling some unsightly dead trunk with its foliage of shining green and its countless clusters of creamy white flowers, it forms one of the most attractive objects imaginable. Thin out its shoots; but do not prune them, since, if they are much shortened, they will yield no flowers whatever. Give it a rich soil, with autumnal top-dressing of manure; a treatment good for the whole group, and, indeed, for all climbing roses. DONNA MARIA has pure white flowers. Its growth is less vigorous than others, its foliage light green, and it blooms in large clusters. MYRIANTHES RÉNONCULE has flowers of a pale peach-color, drooping in large clusters, and in form resembling a double ranunculus. ROSA PLENA is of a bright flesh-color, large and double. PRINCESSE MARIE is reddish-pink. FORTUNE'S YELLOW is a native of China and Japan, and is sometimes included in this class. It is of a bright fawn-color, with a tinge of copper; beautiful under shelter, but will not bear a winter exposure in the Northern States. It is of comparatively recent introduction. RAMPANTE blooms profusely in clusters of pure white. FLORA is of a bright rose; LEOPOLDINE D'ORLÉANS, white, tinged with rose; and SPECTABILIS, rosy-lilac.

While some of this race are perfectly hardy, others will require protection against a Northern winter. The ease of their culture, their rapid growth, and their admirable effect where masses of flowers and verdure are desired, will commend them all to favor in the Middle and Southern States.

"I know of no rose idea," says Mr. Rivers, "prettier than that of a wilderness of evergreen roses, the varieties planted promiscuously, and suffered to cover the surface of the ground with their entangled shoots. To effect this, the ground should be dug, manured, and thoroughly cleaned from perennial weeds, such as couch-grass, &c., and the plants planted from three to five feet asunder. If the soil be rich, the latter distance will do. They must be hoed amongst, and kept clean from weeds after planting, till the branches meet: they will then soon form a beautiful mass of foliage and flowers, covering the soil too densely for weeds of minor growth to flourish. Those weeds that are more robust should be pulled out occasionally; and this is all the culture they will require. For temples, columns, wire-fences, which they soon cover with beauty, and verandas, their use is now becoming well known. One of the most complete temples of roses is that at the seat of —— Warner, Esq., Hoddesdon, Hertfordshire; and the prettiest specimens of festooning these roses from one column to another by means of small iron chains (strong iron wire will do) may be seen at Broxbourn Bury, near Hoddesdon, the seat of —— Bosanquet, Esq.

" . . . About six or eight years ago, I received, among others, some very stout short stocks of the Dog Rose: they were not more than two feet in height, but stouter than a large broom-handle, the bark thick and gray with age. They were planted, and grew most luxuriantly. I was for some little time at a loss what varieties to bud them with; for, be it remembered, all stout and old rose-stocks require to be worked with very strong-growing sorts of roses, to take off the abundance of sap, and keep them in a healthy state. At last, in a mere freak of fancy, I had them budded with some varieties of the Evergreen Rose (*Rosa Sempervirens*). They grew most luxuriantly; and after a year or two, not being trees adapted for sale, they were planted in a sloping bank of strong white clay, and left to grow and bloom as Nature dictated: not a shoot was ever touched with the pruning-knife.

"One of these trees is on a stem a trifle more than two feet in height, and it has been these two or three summers past a picture of beauty. When in full bloom, the ends of its shoots rest on the ground, and it then forms a perfect dome of roses: nothing in rose-culture can really be more beautiful. It will be at once seen with what facility such stout, short, old rose-stocks can be found in any hedge. They may be planted in the kitchen-garden, budded with the above-mentioned sort, and, to give variety in color, with some of the following kinds, — all varieties of Rosa Sempervirens, Myrianthes, Jaunâtre, Adelaide d'Orléans, and Spectabilis. Every bud will succeed, as no roses grow more freely; and, after remaining one season from budding in their 'nursery,' some nice places must be found for them on the lawn, where, unpruned, unchecked, they will, with all the freshness of unassisted Nature, annually delight the eye of the lover of flowers." *

The Multiflora Rose.

Rosa Multiflora. — The parent of this family belongs to Japan and China. With few exceptions, we cannot recommend them to Northern cultivators for growth in the open air, as they bear our winters but indifferently,

---

* This will do for the Southern States. Unhappily, it will not do in New England.

and, in some cases, are killed outright. RUSSELLIANA, or SCARLET GREVILLIA, blooms in large clusters of a rich, dark lake, changing to various shades of red and lilac, so that the cluster presents a curious diversity of hue. As it is extremely vigorous in growth, it would make an admirable pillar or climbing rose, were it but a little more hardy. It would, no doubt, succeed if the pillar were protected during winter by fastening around it a covering of pine or spruce boughs. These exclude sun, but not air; so that the rose is not exposed to the dangers from dampness which attend a compact mass of straw soaked by rain and snow. As RUSSELLIANA bears pruning better than most climbing roses, it may be grown as a bush; in which state it has flourished here for a number of years without protection. DE LA GRIFFERAIE may also be grown as a bush with perfect success as far North as Boston. It gives a great abundance of blush and rose-colored flowers, forming a high mound of bloom. LAURA DAVOUST forms an admirable greenhouse stock for rafter roses. Indeed, it is well worth a place for its own sake. Its small double flowers of bright pink and flesh-color, changing to white, are produced in large and graceful clusters, beautiful from the varieties of shade which they exhibit. CARMIN VELOUTÉ, ALBA, and COCCINEA are also good varieties of this family, the value of which is greatly diminished by the imperfect hardiness of many of its members.

Hybrid Climbing Roses.

The following are roses of doubtful parentage, several of them much esteemed abroad; though, for the most part, they have not been sufficiently tried here to establish their merit and their hardiness in our Northern climate. All those named below bear an English winter.

MADAME D'ARBLAY, or WELLS'S WHITE, is of a light flesh-color, and its growth is exceedingly vigorous. The GARLAND is of a light fawn-color, changing to white, and blooms in large clusters of double flowers, which turn to pink before fading. SIR JOHN SEBRIGHT has small semi-double crimson flowers, a color valuable in a climbing rose, because not very common. MENOUX is also crimson. INDICA MAJOR is of a pale blush. Among others under this head may be mentioned ASTROLABE, BENGALE FORMIDABLE, QUEEN, and CLAIR. The last, however, is but a moderate grower for a climbing rose.

"Among climbing roses, but few can be found that will bear seed in England, the Ayrshire roses excepted, from some of which it is probable that some fine and original climbers may be raised. A most desirable object to obtain is a dark crimson Rosa ruga: this may possibly be accomplished by planting that favorite rose with the Ayrshire Queen, and fertilizing its flowers very carefully with those of that dark rose. It is remarkable, that although these roses are both hybrids, from species apparently very remote in their affinities, yet both of them bear seed, even without being fertilized. The Blush Ayrshire, a most abundant seed-bearer, may also be planted with the Ayrshire Queen, the Gloire de Rosomènes, the Double Yellow Brier, Single Crimson Moss, Celina Moss, the China Rose Fabvier, and its flowers fertilized with the pollen of these roses: if any combination can be effected, pleasing results may reasonably be hoped for. To 'make assurance doubly sure,' the anthers of the Ayrshire Rose should be removed from some of the flowers with which the experiment is tried." — *Rivers.*

Rosa Banksia. — This very beautiful and very singular family more resembles in bloom a double Spiræa prunifolia, dwarf almond, or Chinese plum, than a rose. Its shoots are long, flexible, and graceful, and its foliage of a deep, polished green. In the flowering season, each shoot is like a pendulous garland of white, yellow, or rose-colored blossoms, small in size, and countless in number. It is not hardy here, or even in England; but it is one of the few once-blooming roses that are worth training on a greenhouse rafter. We have found it to succeed in a house without fire, with the protection of straw placed around it in winter. It will then bloom in the spring.

This rose is a native of China, and was named in compliment to Lady Banks. In Italy and the south of France it grows to perfection, climbing with an astonishing vigor, and covering every object within its reach. According to the French writer Deslongchamps, there was in 1842 a Banksia Rose at Toulon, of which the stem was, at its base, two feet and four inches in circumference; while the largest of the six branches measured a foot in girth. Its foliage covered a space of wall seventy-five feet wide, and about eighteen feet high; and it sometimes produced shoots fifteen feet long in a single year. It flowered in April and May; from fifty to sixty thousand of its double white blossoms opening at once, with an effect which the writer describes as magical. This remarkable tree was then about thirty-four years old. Deslongchamps also describes another Banksia Rose at Caserta, in the kingdom of Naples, which climbed to the top of a poplar sixty feet high, killed it with its embraces, and mantled its lifeless form with its rich green drapery, and its flowery garlands and festoons of white.

Banksian roses must not be shortened much; for, if they are, they will not bloom. The branches may be thinned out, however, to any degree necessary. The strong, thick shoots of overgrown proportions, and often but half ripened, which they sometimes make towards the end of summer, should be cut out, as they draw too much life from the blooming part of the plant. The same rule will also apply to many other species. These gross and immature shoots occur in many roses, both in the open ground and under glass; and, as they rarely produce good flowers, they should not be suffered to rob the rest of the plant of its nourishment.

The DOUBLE WHITE BANKSIA is the best known, and one of the most beautiful. JAUNÂTRE PLEINE is of a primrose yellow. JAUNE SERIN is of a bright yellow. FORTUNE'S BANKSIA has double white flowers, much larger than usual with the species, and is greatly admired. The YELLOW BANKSIA is of a bright yellow, small, and very double. ROSEA is of a bright rose, double.

The Banksia is frequently used in greenhouses and conservatories as a stock for other climbing roses; and, in many cases, answers well.

The Prairie Rose.

Rosa Rubifolia. — This native rose has been much improved by Mr. Feast and others, and now has many varieties, some of which are evidently hybrids. The single variety is in itself very attractive; blooming in clusters, which last a long time, and exhibit a pleasing diversity of shade, since the flowers grow paler as they grow old. For our own part, we prefer the parent to most of its more pretending offspring.

All of this family are held in great scorn by transatlantic cultivators. Perhaps the climate of England is unfavorable to them; perhaps national prejudice may color the judgment; or perhaps the fact that a less rigorous climate permits the successful cultivation of many fine climbing roses which cannot well be grown here may explain the slight esteem with which these coarse children of the prairies are regarded. Coarse, without doubt, they are, except those into which another element has been infused by hybridization, accidental or otherwise: and yet our climate forbids us to dispense with them.

The Queen of the Prairies is among those best known and most desirable. Individually, its flowers are as void of beauty as a rose can be. Sometimes they are precisely like a small cabbage, — not the rose so called, but the vegetable, — and they are as deficient in fragrance as in elegance. Yet we regard this rose as a most valuable possession. It will cover a wall, a pillar, a bank, or a dead trunk, with a profusion of bloom, gorgeous as a feature of the garden landscape, though unworthy to be gathered or critically examined. It is perfectly hardy, and of the easiest culture. Those who can make no other rose grow rarely fail with this. The Baltimore Belle is a notable exception to every thing we have said in disparagement of the Prairie roses. It is evidently a hybrid of some tender, ever-blooming variety, apparently one of the Noisettes; and derives, from its paternal parent, qualities of delicacy and beauty which are not conspicuous in the maternal stock. At the same time, it has lost some of the robust and hardy character of the unmixed Prairie. In a severe New-England winter, its younger shoots are often killed back. It shows a tendency to bloom in the autumn; and a trifle more of the Noisette blood infused into it would, no doubt, make it a true autumnal rose. Some florists use it for spring forcing in the greenhouse; for which the delicacy of its clustering white flowers, shaded with a soft, flesh-color, well fits it. When the worthy Rivers, patriarch of English rose-growers, pronounced sentence, *ex cathedrâ*, against the whole race of Prairies, — " I will dismiss them with the remark, that none of them are worth cultivating," — he included in his decree of excommunication one of the prettiest climbing roses in existence.

Anna Maria has very double flowers of pink and rose. Linnæan Hill Beauty bears white and pale blush flowers. Miss Gunnell is pale pink, with a tinge of buff. It is one of the best, though not equal to the Baltimore Belle. Mrs. Hovey has large white flowers; President, deep pink; Triumphant, deep rose; Superba, light pink. Among other sorts are the King of the Prairie, Eva Corinne, Jane, and Seraphim, all excellent for general effect, but not to be classed with the roses suitable for the bouquet or the drawing-room.

The Prairie roses might, no doubt, be greatly improved by hybridizing. Thus, by fertilization with the pollen of the Musk Rose, we should probably obtain an offspring with some of the delicacy and fragrance of that species. Again: by applying the pollen of some vigorous, hardy rose of deep and vivid color, we should improve the color of the Prairie without impairing its hardiness. Hybrid

China Paul Ricaut would probably answer well for this experiment. The Baltimore Belle bears seed occasionally; but is so uncertain and capricious in this respect, that it will require no little perseverance in the hybridist.

AUTUMNAL ROSES. CHAP. VII.

THE ROSES of which we have hitherto spoken have but one period of bloom in the year. June is gay with their flowers; but at midsummer their glory is departed, not again to return till a winter of rest has intervened. Various families of roses have, however, the faculty of continuous or repeated blooming. Some remain in bloom with little interruption for a long time; while others bloom at intervals, after periods of rest. These classes are known, with little discrimination, as " Autumnal Roses," " Ever-blooming Roses," or " Perpetual Roses." The French have a name for those blooming at intervals, which is very appropriate. They call them " Remontant Roses," — *Rosiers Remontants*, — in other words, roses which grow again. This very well describes them. They make a growth in spring and early summer, and the young wood thus produced bears a crop of flowers. Then the plant rests for a while; but soon begins another growth, which, in turn, bears flowers, though less abundantly than before. The June, or once-blooming roses, it is true, make also a first and second growth; but, with them, the second growth gives leaves alone. In the true everblooming roses, or roses that bloom continuously, the growth of young wood capable of bearing flowers is going on with little interruption during the whole period when the vital powers of the plant are awake. It is to stimulate the production of this blooming wood that we prune back the shoots that have already bloomed, as soon as the flowers have faded.

It is the possession of a great variety of roses of repeated or continuous bloom that gives to the rose-lovers of our own day their greatest advantage over those of former times. Our forefathers had but very few autumnal roses. The ancient Romans, it seems, had roses in abundance in November and December; but this must have been with the aid of a supreme skill in cultivation, as there is no reason to believe that they were in possession of those Chinese and Indian species, to which the modern florist is indebted, directly or indirectly, for nearly all his autumnal flowers. As these species are by far the most important of the ever-blooming and *remontant* families, both in themselves and in the numberless progeny of hybrids to whom they have transmitted their qualities, we place them first on our list.

The Chinese Rose.

Rosa Indica. — *Rosa Semperflorens.* — We include under the head of the Chinese Rose two botanical species, because they are so much alike, that, for floral purposes, it is not worth while to separate them, and because their respective offspring are often wholly undistinguishable. The most marked distinction between the two is the greater depth and vividness of the color of Rosa Semperflorens; though, by a singular freak of Nature, seedlings perfectly white are said to have been produced from it.

China roses will not endure our winters without very careful protection; yet they bloom so constantly and so abundantly, that they are very desirable in a garden. In large English pleasure-grounds, they are sometimes planted in masses, each of a distinct color. They may also be so used here by those who will take the trouble to remove them from the ground in the autumn, and place them in a frame for protection. For this purpose, a hot-bed frame may be used, substantially made of plank. It should be placed in a situation where the soil is thoroughly drained either by Nature or Art. The roses are to be placed in it close together, and overlapping each other, to save room; the roots being well covered with soil, and the plants laid in a sloping position. By covering them with boards and mats, they will then be safe from every thing but mice. The most effectual way to defeat the mischievous designs of these pestiferous vermin is to cover, not the roots only, but the entire plants, with earth. The covering of boards and mats must be so placed as to exclude water from rain and melting snow. Tea roses, of which we shall speak under the next head, are, as a class, more tender than the Chinas; and, in order to preserve them, the soil in the frame should be dug out to the depth of a foot, the roses laid at the bottom, and wholly covered with earth somewhat dry. On this earth, after the roses are buried, place a covering of dry leaves some six inches deep, and then cover the whole with water-proof boards or sashes. The leaves alone, if in sufficient quantity, would protect the roses from cold, but, at the same time, afford a tempting harborage for mice, which would destroy the plants, unless buried out of their reach. Thus treated, the tenderest Tea roses will bear the winter with impunity in the coldest parts of New England.

Though China roses are not equal in beauty to some of their hybrid offspring to be hereafter described, they surpass all other roses for pot-culture in the window of the parlor or drawing-room. They are more easily managed than Tea roses, and, though less fragrant, are not less abundant in bloom. No roses are of easier culture in the greenhouse. The varieties of this group are the Bengal roses of the French, and are those familiarly known among us as Monthly roses. They were introduced into England from the East about the beginning of the last century.

CARMIN D'YÈBLES, or CARMIN SUPERBE, has bright carmine flowers. CRAMOISIE SUPÉRIEURE has double crimson flowers, and, like the former, is excellent for pot-culture. EUGÈNE BEAUHARNAIS is large, very double, and of a bright amaranth-color, approaching crimson. FABVIER is of crimson scarlet, very vivid and striking. PRESIDENT D'OLBÉQUE is of a cherry-red.

All of the above belong to the Semperflorens species, and are of deep colors. The following are varieties of

Rosa Indica. ARCHDUKE CHARLES is of a bright rose-color, gradually deepening as the flower grows older, till it becomes, at times, almost crimson. CELS MULTIFLORA is white, shaded with pink, and flowers very freely. MADAME BRÉON is of a rich rose-color, very large, double, and compact in form. CLARA SYLVAIN is pure white. MADAME BUREAU is white, with a faint tinge of straw-color. MRS. BOSANQUET may be placed in this division; for, though it is certainly a hybrid, the blood of the China Rose predominates in it, and characterizes it. It is of a pale, waxy, flesh color, very delicate and beautiful, at the same time large and double. NAPOLÉON is of a bright pink, and the DUCHESS OF KENT is white.

The Dwarf roses, called Lawrenceanas, or Fairy roses, are varieties of the Chinese. They are very small, many of them not exceeding a foot in height, and are used as edging for flower-beds in countries of which the climate is not too severe for them. Like all other China roses, they are very easily grown in pots.

"China roses are better adapted than almost any other class for forming groups of separate colors. Thus, for beds of white roses, — which, let it be remembered, will bloom constantly from June till October, — Clara Sylvain and Madame Bureau are beautiful. The former is the taller grower, and should be planted in the centre of the bed. For crimson, take Cramoisie Supérieure, — no other variety approaches this in its peculiar richness of color; for scarlet, Fabvier; for red, Prince Charles and Carmin Superbe; for deep crimson, Eugène Beauharnais; for blush, Mrs. Bosanquet; for a variegated group, changeable as the chameleon, take Archduke Charles and Virginie; for rose, Madame Bréon. I picture to myself the above on a well-kept lawn, their branches pegged to the ground so as to cover the entire surface; and can scarcely imagine any thing more chaste and beautiful.

"To succeed in making these roses bear and ripen their seed in England, a warm, dry soil and south wall are necessary; or, if the plants can be trained to a flued wall, success will be more certain. Eugène Beauharnais, fertilized with Fabvier, would probably produce first-rate brilliant-colored flowers. Archduke Charles, by removing a few of the small central petals, just before their flowers are expanded, and fertilizing it with pollen from Fabvier or Henry the Fifth, would give seed; and as the object ought to be, in this family, to have large flowers with brilliant colors, and plants of hardy, robust habits, no better union can be formed. China roses, if blooming in an airy greenhouse, will often produce fine seed: by fertilizing their flowers, it may probably be insured. In addition, therefore, to those planted against a wall, some strong plants of the above varieties should be planted in the orchard-house, — the place, above all others, adapted for seed-bearing roses." — *Rivers.*

The Tea Scented Rose.

Rosa Indica Odorata. — This is a Chinese species, closely allied to the last named, but more beautiful, far more fragrant, and usually more tender. The two original varieties of it, the Blush Tea and the Yellow Tea, were introduced into England early in the present century; and between them they have produced a numerous family, than which no roses are more beautiful.

To grow them in the open air, they require, in the first place, a very thorough drainage. If the situation is at all damp, the bed should be raised some six inches above the surrounding surface; but this will be rarely necessary in our climate. If it rests on a good natural stratum of gravel, this will be drainage sufficient; but, if not, the whole bed should be excavated, and underlaid to the depth of four or five inches with broken stones, broken bricks, or with what is much better than either, — oyster-shells. Over these, sift coarse gravel to prevent the soil from working into their crevices, and on the gravel make a bed somewhat more than a foot deep of good loam, mixed with a nearly equal quantity of light, well-rotted manure, adding sand if the texture of the loam requires it. The bed should be in an open, sunny situation, and sheltered, as far as may be, from strong winds. The Tea roses planted in it — unless they have been exhausted by forcing in the greenhouse — will give a liberal supply of bloom until checked by the autumn frosts.

Many of these roses can be grown to great advantage in a cold grapery, in a bed suitably prepared. They differ greatly in hardiness, and in respect to ease of culture. Some are so vigorous as to form greenhouse climbers, and so hardy as to bear a Northern winter by being simply laid down, and covered with earth, like a raspberry. Of these is GLOIRE DE DIJON, a rose of most vigorous growth, and closely resembling in the shape of its blossoms that matchless Bourbon Rose, the well-known Souvenir de la Malmaison. Its color, however, is very different, being a mixture of buff and salmon. It has one defect, — a crumpled appearance of the central leaves, which gives them a somewhat withered look, even when just open. Five or six large plants of this variety are growing here with the utmost luxuriance on the rafters of a glass house, without fire. In winter they are protected by meadow-hay thrust between them and the glass, and have never been injured by the frost.

For preserving a small number of Tea roses through the winter, an ordinary cellar answers perfectly, provided there is no furnace in it. They may either be potted or "heeled" in earth in a box. A few degrees of frost will not hurt them. Roses and all other plants will bear the same degree of cold much better in a close, still air than in the open sunlight and wind.

The prevailing colors of Tea roses are light and delicate: of the rose-colored varieties, ADAM is one of the finest, as is also SOUVENIR D'UN AMI. MOIRET is of a pale yellow, shaded with fawn and rose. BOUGÈRE is of a deep rosy bronze, large and double. SILÈNE resembles it in color, and is very much admired. CANARY is of the color which its name indicates, and its buds are extremely beautiful. Yet, in this respect, no variety can exceed the OLD YELLOW TEA, which is, however, one of the most tender and difficult of culture in the whole group. DEVONIENSIS is very large, double, and of a pale clear yellow; a very fine rose, but shy of bloom. GLOIRE DE DIJON, already mentioned, is a superb rose, though somewhat wanting in that grace and delicacy, which, in general, characterize this class. MADAME BRAVY is of a creamy white, and very beautifully formed. MADAME DAMAIZIN is salmon, and very free in bloom. MADAME WILLIAM is of a bright yellow, large, and very double. NIPHETOS is of a pale lemon, turning to snow-white. SAFRANO is one of the most distinct and remarkable roses in the group. It is of a buff and apricot hue, altogether peculiar. Its buds are beautifully formed; as are also its half-opened flowers, though they are not very double. It is a very profuse bloomer, easy of culture, free of growth, and hardy as compared with most other Tea roses.

"With attention, some very beautiful roses of this family may be originated from seed; but the plants must be trained against a south wall, in a warm, dry soil, or grown in pots, under glass. A warm greenhouse or the orchard-house will be most proper for them, so that they bloom in May, as their hips are a long time ripening.

"For yellow roses, Vicomtesse Decazes may be planted with and fertilized by Canary, which abounds in pollen: some fine roses, almost to a certainty, must be raised from seed produced by such a union. For the sake of curiosity, a few flowers of the latter might be fertilized with the Double Yellow Brier, or Rosa Harrisonii. The Old Yellow Tea Rose bears seed abundantly; but it has been found from repeated experiments that a good or even a mediocre rose is seldom or never produced from it: but, fertilized with the Yellow Brier, something original may be realized. Souvenir d'un Ami and Adam would produce seed of fine quality, from which large and bright rose-colored varieties might be expected; Niphetos would give pure white Tea roses; and Gloire de Dijon, fertilized with Safrano, would probably originate first-rate fawn-colored roses: but the central petals of the latter should be carefully removed with tweezers or pliers, as its flowers are too double for it to be a certain seed-bearer."—*Rivers.*

The Musk Rose.

Rosa Moschata.—This rose is a native of Asia, Northern Africa, and adjacent islands. In Persia it is said to reach a prodigious size, resembling some gorgeous flowering tree. It is said, too, that it is the favorite rose of the Persian poets, who celebrated its loves with the nightingale in strains echoed by their English imitators. Being very vigorous, it is best grown as a climber; but, with us, it requires the shelter of glass. It flowers in large clusters late in summer, and in a warm, moist air, exhales a faint odor of musk.

The DOUBLE WHITE MUSK has yellowish white flowers of moderate size. EPONINE has pure white flowers, very double. The NEW DOUBLE WHITE, or RANUNCULUS

Musk, is an improvement on the Double White, which it much resembles. Nivea, or the Snowy Musk, can hardly be said to belong to the group, as it blooms only once in the year. Ophir, Princess of Nassau, and Rivers, are also good examples of this family.

The Noisette Rose.

Rosa Moschata Hybrida.— Having treated of the China, Tea, and Musk roses, we now come to the hybrid offspring which they have jointly produced. In 1817, M. Noisette, a French florist at Charleston, S.C., raised a seedling from the Musk Rose, impregnated with the pollen of the common China Rose. The seedling was different from either parent, but had the vigorous growth of the Musk Rose, together with its property of blooming in clusters, and a slight trace of its peculiar fragrance. This was the original Noisette Rose, and it has been the parent of a numerous family; but as it has, in turn, been fertilized with the pollen of the Tea, and perhaps of other roses, many of its descendants have lost its peculiar characteristics, so that in some cases they cannot be distinguished from Tea roses. It is thus that confusion is constantly arising in all the families of the rose; the groups becoming merged in each other by insensible gradations, so that it is impossible to fix any clear line of demarcation between them.

The distinctive characteristic of the true Noisette is blooming in clusters. Different varieties have different habits of growth, some being much more vigorous than others; but the greater part are true climbing roses. Those in which the blood of the Musk and China predominate are comparatively hardy. Many of them can be grown as bushes in the open air, with very little winter protection, even in the latitude of Boston. Two varieties — Madame Massot and Caroline Marniesse — are to-day (Oct. 16) in full bloom here, where they have stood for several years, with very little precaution to shelter them. Some other varieties, again, strongly impregnated with the Tea Rose, are quite as tender as Tea roses of the pure race.

As rafter-roses in the greenhouse, the Noisettes are unsurpassed.

AIMÉE VIBERT is one of the prettiest of the group. It was raised by the French cultivator Vibert, who named it after his daughter. The flowers are pure white, and grow in large clusters. Though not among the most vigorous in growth of the Noisettes, this variety is comparatively hardy, and in all respects very desirable. MISS GLEGG resembles her French sister, but is scarcely so graceful or elegant. JOAN OF ARC is a pure white rose, growing very vigorously. MADAME MASSOT, sometimes sold by American nursery-men under the name of MADEMOISELLE HENRIETTE, bears large clusters of small flowers of a waxy white, faintly tinged with flesh-color. It is one of the hardiest of the group. CAROLINE MARNIESSE somewhat resembles it, but is not equal in beauty.

All of the above have very distinctly the Noisette characteristics, as inherited from their parent, the Musk Rose. Those which follow have been hybridized to such a degree with the Tea Rose, that its traits predominate; and though, in some of them, the cluster-blooming habit of the Musk is not lost, the flowers bear, in size, shape, color, and fragrance, a marked resemblance to the Tea. CHROMATELLA, or the CLOTH OF GOLD, is, when in perfection, the most beautiful of all the yellow roses; but it is shy of bloom, and difficult of culture. SOLFATERRE is also a fine yellow rose, much more easily managed than the last. The same may be said of AUGUSTA, a seedling raised from it in this country. ISABELLA GRAY was also raised in America, and is a seedling from the Cloth of Gold, which it rivals in beauty; though, like its parent, it is somewhat difficult to manage. JAUNE DESPREZ, or DESPREZ'S YELLOW, is of a sulphur-color tinged with red, very large and fragrant. AMERICA is also a large and fine flower of a creamy white; but perhaps the best known of the whole group is LAMARQUE, in New England the greatest favorite among greenhouse climbers. Its flowers are of a sulphur-yellow, large and double; and its growth is very vigorous.

"But few of the Noisette roses will bear seed in this country: the following, however, if planted against a south wall, and carefully fertilized, would probably produce some. The object here should be to obtain dark crimson varieties with large flowers; and for this purpose Fellenberg should be fertilized with Octavie, Solfaterre with the Tea Rose. Vicomtesse Decazes would probably give yellow varieties; and these would be large and fragrant, as in Lamarque and Jaune Desprez. In these directions for procuring seed from roses by fertilizing, I have confined myself to such varieties as are almost sure to produce it; but much must be left to the amateur, as many roses may be made fertile by removing their central petals, and consequently some varieties that I have not noticed may be made productive."— *Rivers.*

The Damask Perpetual Rose.

Rosa Damascena. — This is a race of Damask roses endowed with the faculty of blooming in the autumn. The old roses known as the Monthly (not the China roses so called) and the Four Seasons are the parents of the group, though not without some infusion of foreign blood. The Damask Perpetuals are hardy, and remarkable for fragrance. They demand rich culture, even more than most other roses; and the best of them with neglect and low diet will bloom but once in the year, and that indifferently. On the other hand, they repay generous treatment liberally, as some of them are as beautiful as they are fragrant. American nursery-men usually catalogue them among the Hybrid Perpetuals, where they are out of place; since the true Damask Perpetual is not, in any sense, a hybrid, though, as before mentioned, some foreign blood has found its way into the family.

The French rose-grower Vibert has formed a new group, which he calls the Rose de Trianon, out of the Damask Perpetuals; but, as the subdivision seems unnecessary and perplexing, we shall re-annex it to the parent group.

The following are good examples of these Perpetuals: JOASINE HANET has deep purplish-red flowers, very showy. SYDONIE bears large flowers of a rose or bright salmon, and blooms profusely. YOLANDE OF ARAGON has deep-pink flowers, and is an abundant autumn bloomer. The above belong to Vibert's new division. The following are unquestioned Damask: CRIMSON, or ROSE DU ROI, is of a bright crimson, very large, very fragrant, and an excellent autumn bloomer. There is a history attached to it. Count Lelieur was superintendent of the royal gardens of St. Cloud, where this rose was raised from seed, a little before the restoration of the Bourbons. He named it Rose Lelieur, after himself. When Louis the Eighteenth came to the throne, an officer of his household insisted that the new rose should be named after him. Count Lelieur resisted. A debate ensued. The party of the courtiers prevailed: the new rose was called the King's Rose, *Rose du Roi;* and the count resigned his post in disgust. MOGADOR is a seedling from this rose, and is, perhaps, an improvement on it. PORTLAND BLANCHE is pure white, and blooms well in autumn. An English writer sets it down as worthless: whence I infer that there must be two of the same name; for here it has proved itself one of the most beautiful of white roses. BERNARD is a small but very beautiful rose, of a clear salmon-color, and is said to be a sport from the Crimson.

"As the culture of this class of roses," says Rivers, "is at present but imperfectly understood, I shall give the result of my experience as to their cultivation, with suggestions to be acted upon according to circumstances. One peculiar feature they nearly all possess,—a reluctance to root when layered: consequently, Perpetual Damask roses, on their own roots, will always be scarce. When it is possible to procure them, they will be found to flourish much better on dry, poor soils than when budded, as at present. These roses require a superabundant quantity of food: it is therefore perfectly ridiculous to plant them on dry lawns, to suffer the grass to grow close up to their stems, and not to give them a particle of manure for years. Under these circumstances, the best varieties, even the Rose du Roi, will scarcely ever give a second series of flowers. To remedy the inimical nature of dry soils to this class of roses, an annual application of manure on the surface of the soil is quite necessary. The ground must not be dug, but lightly pricked over with a fork in November; after which some manure must be laid on, about two or three inches in depth, which ought not to be disturbed, except to clean with the hoe and rake, till the following autumn. This, in some situations, in the spring months, will be unsightly: in such cases, cover with some nice green moss, as directed in the culture of Hybrid China roses. I have said that this treatment is applicable to dry, poor soils: but, even in good rose soils, it is almost necessary; for it will give such increased vigor, and such a prolongation of the flowering season, as amply to repay the labor bestowed. If the soil be prepared as directed, they will twice in the year require pruning: in November [*in March, for this country*], when the beds are dressed; and again in the beginning of June. In the November pruning, cut off from every shoot of the preceding summer's growth about two-thirds its length: if they are crowded, remove some of them entirely. If this autumnal pruning is attended to, there will be, early in June the following summer, a vast number of luxuriant shoots, each crowned with a cluster of buds. Now, as June roses are always abundant, a little sacrifice must be made to insure a fine autumnal bloom: therefore leave only half the number of shoots to bring forth their summer flowers; the remainder shorten to about half their length. Each shortened branch will soon put forth buds; and in August and September the plants will again be covered with flowers. In cultivating Perpetual roses of all classes, the faded flowers ought immediately to be removed; for in autumn the petals do not fall off readily, but lose their color, and remain on the plant, to the injury of the forthcoming buds. Though I have recommended them to be grown on their own roots, in dry soils, yet, on account of the autumnal rains dashing the dirt upon their flowers when close to the ground, wherever it is possible to make budded roses grow, they ought to be preferred; for, on stems from one to two feet in height, the flowers will not be soiled: they are also brought near to the eye, and the plant forms a neat and pretty object."

THE BOURBON ROSE.

Rosa Hybrida Bourboniensis. — The China Rose and one of the old Damask Perpetuals, known as the Red Four Seasons, have produced between them a distinct family of hybrids known as the Bourbon roses. They are so called because they were originated on the Isle of Bourbon. One M. Perichon, an inhabitant of that island, in planting a quantity of seedling roses raised for a hedge, found one very different from the rest, and planted it apart. On flowering, it proved to be distinct from any rose before known. Soon after, in the year 1817, a French botanist, M. Bréon, arriving at the Isle of Bourbon as curator of the government botanical garden established there, investigated the case of this remarkable seedling, and became convinced that it was produced between the two species named above; since these were then the only roses on the island, and both were freely used as hedges. M.

Bréon sent plants and seeds of the new rose to Paris; and from these have sprung the whole race of the Bourbons,—a race of sweeter savor in horticulture than in history.

They are remarkable as a family for clearness and brightness of color, perfection of form, and freedom of autumnal blooming. Some of them are quite hardy; others are not so in New England. Their growth is various; some climbing vigorously if trained to do so, and others forming compact bushes. Abundance of manure, a deep and well-dug soil, and mulching with newly-cut grass or some similar substance to keep them moist in dry weather, joined to judicious pruning, are needed to bring forth their beauties in perfection. The stronger growers cannot be pruned severely without greatly diminishing the quantity of their bloom; but the ends of tall, strong shoots of the same season's growth may be cut off with great advantage, thus checking their growth, and causing them to throw out small blooming side-shoots.

No roses are better than these where the object is to produce a late autumnal bloom. They may be made to bloom into the winter by pinching off their summer flower-buds, in order that they may not exhaust themselves in that season, and by sheltering them from the frost. For forcing, they are unsurpassed.

Some of the most vigorous varieties would make gorgeous pillar-roses, provided pains were taken to lay them flat, and cover them with earth every winter. Without protection, they would suffer severely in the Northern States.

ACIDALIE was, till recently, the only white Bourbon; yet it is not pure white, but has a tinge of blush. Of late, another white Bourbon has been added, — BLANCHE LAFITTE, — which is also faintly tinged with flesh-color. ADELAIDE BOUGÈRE is of a rich velvety purple. DUPETIT THOUARS is of a vivid crimson, large and double. GEORGE PEABODY is of a purplish-crimson. LOUISE ODIER is a rose of very vigorous growth, and one of the hardier members of the family: its flowers are of a bright rose-color, of a beautiful cupped form; and it has a tendency to bloom in clusters. PRINCE ALBERT is still hardier. Its color is a brilliant crimson-scarlet, and its autumn bloom is abundant. SIR JOSEPH PAXTON is of a bright rose-color, tinged with crimson: its growth is exceedingly vigorous; and, with moderate protection, it will bear our winters. SOUVENIR DE LA MALMAISON is unsurpassed among roses. It is very large, and beautifully formed. It is of a light, transparent flesh-color; and no rose is more admired in a greenhouse. It will also thrive in the open air, and, when the soil is well drained, may safely be trusted to bear a New-England winter, provided it is covered with earth. In a wet soil, it is usually killed. VORACE is of a dark purplish-crimson, and, like the last named, only partially hardy. HERMOSA, or ARMOSA, resembles a China rose in the character and abundance of its bloom. None surpasses it for forcing.

The above will serve as favorable examples of the best types of this group.

"I hope in a few years to see Bourbon roses in every garden; for 'the Queen of Flowers' boasts no member of her court more beautiful. Their fragrance also is delicate and pleasing, more particularly in the autumn. They ought to occupy a distinguished place in the autumnal rose-garden, in clumps or beds, as standards and as pillars. In any and in all situations, they must and will please. To insure a very late autumnal bloom, a collection of dwarf standards, *i.e.* stems one to two feet in height, should be potted in large pots, and, during summer, watered with manure-water, and some manure kept on the surface. Towards the end of September or the middle of October, if the weather be wet, they may be placed under glass. They will bloom in fine perfection even as late as November. . . .

"It is difficult to point out roses of this family that bear seed freely, except the Common Bourbon; but Acidalie, planted against a south wall, would probably give some seed.* If any pollen can be found, it might be fertilized with the flowers of Julie de Loynes. A pure white and true Bourbon Rose ought to be the object: therefore it should not be hybridized with any other species. Bouquet de Flore may be planted against a south wall with Menoux, with which it should be carefully fertilized: some interesting varieties may be expected from seed thus produced. Queen of the Bourbons, planted with the yellow China Rose, might possibly give some seeds; but those would not produce true Bourbon roses, as the former is a hybrid, partaking of the qualities of the Tea-scented roses. Anne Beluze, planted with Madame Nérard, would give seed from which some very delicate Blush roses might be raised; and Le Florifère, fertilized with the Common Bourbon, would also probably produce seed worthy of attention." — *Rivers.*

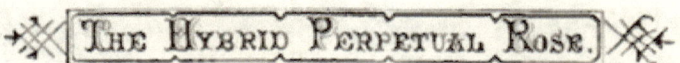

The Hybrid Perpetual Rose.

We reach, at length, the vast family of the Hybrid Perpetuals, — a race of brilliant *parvenus*, which, within the last twenty-five years, have risen to throw other roses into

---

* In America, several varieties bear seed well. Sir Joseph Paxton rarely fails, and is a very good subject for experiment. The varieties named above by Mr. Rivers are not, for the most part, of the first merit.

the shade. As we look upon them, we survey a gorgeous chaos. Here are innumerable varieties of foliage and flower, perplexing us in our search for genealogies and relationships. All of them, however, have, as a basis, some hardy, once-blooming rose, with which has been mingled the blood of one, and often of many, of the ever-blooming roses, in sufficient proportion to impart some of their qualities of autumnal flowering. Many of the Hybrid Perpetuals have, as their basis, the Hybrid China Rose, already described under the head of the summer roses. This, as we have seen, blooms but once; but when crossed with the China, Tea, Bourbon, Damask Perpetual, or several of these combined, it becomes capable of blooming in the autumn, without losing its hardiness. Such, then, is the origin of this group; and the diversity of its characteristics answers to the diversity of its parentage. Thus two roses can scarcely be more unlike than Baronne Prévost and the Giant of Battles, or La Reine and Arthur de Sansal. In Baronne Prévost and La Reine, the hardier and more vigorous elements prevail; and they probably owe their ever-blooming qualities to an infusion of the Damask Perpetual, rather than of the more tender China roses. In the Giant of Battles and Arthur de Sansal, on the contrary, the China and Bourbon elements are very apparent; and, while these roses are excellent autumn bloomers, they are much less hardy and vigorous than the other two.

M. Laffay, in his garden at Bellevue, a few miles from Paris, may be said to have laid the foundations of the Hybrid Perpetual family. Indeed, to a great extent, he created it; having originated a great number of beautiful roses, some of which none of the more recent productions have been able in the least degree to eclipse. Laffay's roses were chiefly of the hardier and stronger type, with La Reine, which was produced about the year 1840, at their head.

From the motley character of the group, the lines that separate it from the Bourbon and from some other families cannot be definitely drawn; and there are certain varieties which always hold an equivocal position, being sometimes placed with one group, and sometimes with another.

These Perpetuals differ greatly in the freedom of their autumn blooming; some giving a second and third crop of flowers in abundance; while others will not bloom at all after midsummer, except under careful and skilful treatment. All require rich culture and good pruning. When an abundant autumn bloom is required, a portion of the June bloom must be sacrificed by cutting back about half the flower-stems to three or four eyes as soon as the flower-buds form. When the flowers fade, these also should be cut off with the stems that bear them, in a similar manner. The formation of the seed-vessels, by employing the vitality of the plant, tends greatly to diminish its autumn bloom. Give additional manure every year, and keep the ground open, and free of weeds. If rank, strong shoots, full of redundant sap, form in summer, check their disproportioned growth by cutting off their tops.

In the North, these roses are better for a little winter protection, such as earthing them up at the base, or thrusting pine-boughs into the soil among them. They may with great advantage be taken up as often as once in three years, and replanted after two or three shovelfuls of old manure have been dug into the soil, which, at the same time, should be forked to the greatest possible depth. Indeed, it does them no harm to replant them yearly: on the contrary, they generally bloom the better for it.

An excellent way to preserve them during winter, when they have been taken out of the ground, is to bury them, root and branch, in earth. The earth for this purpose should not be very moist. The place selected should be sheltered and dry; the latter point being of the last importance. The roses may be tied in bundles, and the earth thrown over them to the depth of six inches or more, in such a manner as to shed the rain and snow; and if a few boards are placed over it, in a sloping position, it will be so much the better. In this way, all the half-hardy roses, and many of those regarded as the most tender, can be safely wintered in the coldest parts of New England.

It is to the family of Hybrid Perpetuals that the French rose-growers have given their chief attention. Hence an enormous multiplication of varieties, every year bringing forth a new brood, perplexing us with their numbers, and by the clamor with which the merits of each and all are proclaimed by their respective originators. Some of these new roses are unsurpassed in beauty, and deserve all that can be said of them. Yet thoroughly to establish the character of a rose requires several years, — not less than six, according to the eminent French rose-grower, M. Jules Margottin: therefore it is impossible to speak with entire confidence of these novelties. I shall begin with roses of well-established merit, which have been for years in cultivation here. Of the rest, which have had not more than a season's trial, mention will be made afterwards.

La Reine is perhaps entitled to the first mention, as it

was one of the first in its origin, and has never since lost ground. It varies very much in quality with circumstances of soil and cultivation, and in its color is surpassed by many other roses. Its very large size when well grown, its fine form and perfect hardiness, are its points of merit. It is the mother of a numerous progeny, among which Auguste Mie is one of the best, growing very vigorously, and bearing flowers equal to those of its parent in beauty of form, and superior in delicacy of color. They are of a fine rose-color, several shades lighter than that of La Reine. Louise Peyronney, also, in many respects, surpasses her parent; and is a rose of great beauty, though scarcely so vigorous as La Reine. Baronne Prévost is another hardy and vigorous rose, of a type wholly different: it grows with great vigor, bears the rudest winter, and, both in June and in the autumnal months, yields an abundance of large, very double flowers of a light rose-color. Pius IX. has the same vigor of constitution, and the same abundant bloom: its flowers are of a deep rose, tinged with crimson. Dr. Arnold is of a deeper color, approaching to crimson, and is one of the best autumn bloomers. Madame Boll is a superb rose, very vigorous, very hardy, and very double. L'Enfant du Mt. Carmel somewhat resembles it, but grows and blooms more freely:

its color is a rosy crimson. JULES MARGOTTIN has no superior in its way: it is of a clear, rosy-crimson color, and its half-opened buds are especially beautiful. TRIOMPHE DE L'EXPOSITION is of a deep crimson; and SOUVENIR DE LA REINE D'ANGLETERRE, of a bright rose: both are very vigorous and very effective. GENERAL JACQUEMINOT is of a fine crimson, and, though not perfectly double, is, nevertheless, one of the most splendid of roses. Its size, under good culture, is immense. It is a strong grower and abundant bloomer, and glows like a firebrand among the paler hues around it. It is one of the hardier kinds, and is easily managed. Its offspring are innumerable. The greater part of the new roses of the last year or two own it as a parent, and inherit some of its qualities. Of its older progeny, TRIOMPHE DES BEAUX ARTS and the ORIFLAMME DE ST. LOUIS may be mentioned with honor. The last, especially, is a very brilliant rose. Among other deep-colored roses are TRIOMPHE DE PARIS, GLOIRE DE SANTENAY, and GENERAL WASHINGTON; the last a seedling from Triomphe de l'Exposition. It is a new rose; but there can be little doubt of its merit.

Perhaps no rose among the Hybrid Perpetuals has been so famous, and so much praised, as the GIANT OF BATTLES; but we cannot fully echo the commendations bestowed upon it. All the roses just named are hardy, vigorous, and of easy culture, available to the half-practised amateur as well as to the experienced cultivator. But the class of Hybrid Perpetuals of which the Giant of Battles is the type, and, to a great extent, the parent, requires more skill and precaution for successful culture. They are all more or less liable to mildew. "I can do nothing with the Giant, because the mildew destroys it," a well-known nursery-man writes me. Besides this tendency, it is by no means of the vigorous growth which the catalogues of nursery-men commonly ascribe to it. Its flowers, however, are very brilliant, and, in a favorable season, are produced in abundance. In color, they resemble those of General Jacqueminot. Some of the seedlings raised from them are much darker; and among these may be mentioned ARTHUR DE SANSAL, CARDINAL PATRIZZI, and the EMPEROR OF MOROCCO. LORD RAGLAN is one of the very finest flowers of this section; and the plant is more vigorous, and less liable to mildew, than the rest of the group.

The following are of the lighter and more delicate shades: CAROLINE DE SANSAL is of a clear flesh-color, large, full, and of a vigorous, hardy constitution. MADAME VIDOT is, when in perfection, an exquisite rose, of a transparent, waxy, flesh color, and formed like a camellia: it has not proved hardy here, and has suffered severely every winter. QUEEN VICTORIA is of a better constitution: it is white, shaded with pink. WILLIAM GRIFFITHS is an old and excellent rose, of a peculiar light satin rose-color: it rarely suffers from the winter. VIRGINAL is pure white. LA MÈRE DE ST. LOUIS is of a waxy flesh-color, and, though not very full, is distinct and beautiful. MADAME RIVERS is of a very light rose. COMTESSE DE CHABRILLANT is of a clear pink, and very fine. MADAME KNORR is of a somewhat deeper shade, and singularly beautiful in bud. LOUISE MAGNAN and DR. HENON may, with Virginal, in the absence of better, represent the white Hybrid Perpetuals, — a color in which this class is very deficient; while a yellow or buff rose is as yet unknown in it, although it is said that such an one has been produced, and will soon be "brought out."

The following are a selection from the new roses; and, though their merits have not as yet been tried by the test of time, there can be very little doubt that all of them will prove of the highest merit:—

MAURICE BERNARDIN is of a bright vermilion, very large and full. CHARLES LEFEBVRE is of a bright crimson, purplish at the centre, and seems an admirable rose. MRS. WILLIAM PAUL is of a violet-red, shaded with crimson.

Madame Clémence Joigneaux is of a red and lilac color, and grows with great vigor. Lord Macaulay is of a rich scarlet-crimson: a bloom of it is now before me, cut here, in the open air, on the 22d of October. Sœur des Anges owes its singular name to the delicacy of its tint, — a soft flesh-color; yet the habit of the plant is vigorous, and it seems of a hardy nature. Duc de Rohan is red, shaded with vermilion. Beauty of Waltham, an English seedling like Lord Macaulay, is of a bright carmine, and blooms profusely. Madame Furtado is very large, fragrant, and double: its color is a light rosy-crimson. Le Rhone is of a brilliant and deep vermilion. Duc de Cazes is of a purplish crimson, so deep as almost to appear black. President Lincoln is cherry-red. Princess of Wales is a recent seedling of Mr. William Paul, the English rose-grower; and, though I have not yet seen it in flower, it is so highly extolled by an English amateur, that I mention it here. It is of a bright crimson, with thick and firm petals, and said to be very hardy. Senateur Vaisse is of a brilliant red, and has found numerous admirers. Victor Verdier is carmine, shaded with purple, large and showy. Louise Margottin is of a delicate, glossy rose-color, beautifully formed; and, though marked of moderate growth on foreign catalogues, it has grown with uncommon vigor here. PRINCE CAMILLE DE ROHAN is of a deep maroon approaching crimson. It is very large and full.

The above comprise the flowers of most brilliant promise among the recent novelties. Many others will be mentioned in the supplementary list.

The Hybrid Perpetuals combine merits so numerous and so brilliant, that they are rapidly driving out of cultivation many roses once in the highest esteem. Indeed, with the exception of Moss roses, and some of the Teas, Noisettes, and Bourbons, none seem likely to maintain their ground before these gorgeous upstarts, some of which are as robust as they are beautiful. Their beauties, however, depend greatly on their culture; and this is true of all roses. A rose which, under indifferent treatment, will be passed unnoticed, puts on, in the hands of a good cultivator, its robes of royalty, and challenges from all beholders the homage due to the Queen of Flowers.

In conclusion, the amateur will do well to make this his golden rule: *Cultivate none but the best, and cultivate them thoroughly.* Thoroughness is at the bottom of all horticultural success.

"Raising new varieties of this family from seed presents an extensive field of interest to the amateur; for we have yet to add to our catalogues pure white and yellow and fawn-colored Hybrid Perpetuals: and these, I anticipate, will be the reward of those who persevere. Monsieur Laffay, by persevering through two or three generations, obtained a mossy Hybrid Bourbon rose, and many of the finest varieties described in the foregoing pages. This information will, I trust, be an incentive to amateurs in this country. To illustrate this, I may here remark, that a yellow Ayrshire Rose, now a desideratum, must not be expected from the first trial; but probably a climbing rose, tinged with yellow or buff, may be the fruit of the first crossing. This variety must again be crossed with a yellow rose: the second generation will, perhaps, be nearer the end wished for. Again: the amateur must bring perseverance and skill into action; and then, if in the third generation a bright yellow climbing rose be obtained, its possession will amply repay the labor bestowed. But these light gardening operations are not labor: they are a delightful amusement to a refined mind, and lead it to reflect on the wonderful infinities of Nature.

"Madame Laffay is an excellent seed-bearing rose: this may be fertilized with the Bourbon Gloire de Rosomènes and with Comte Bobrinsky. Dr. Marx may be crossed with the Bourbon Paul Joseph and with the Bourbon Le Grenadier. These should all be planted against a south wall, so that their flowers expand at the same time; and they will probably give some fine autumnal roses, brilliant in color, and very double. For fawn-colored, or yellowish and white roses, Duchess of Sutherland may be fertilized with the Tea-scented roses Victoria and Safrano. These must all have a south wall. These hints may possibly be considered meagre and incomplete; but I trust it will be seen how much depends upon the enterprise and taste of the cultivator." — *Rivers.*

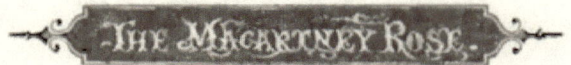
The Macartney Rose.

Rosa Bracteata. — The original species was brought to England from China by Lord Macartney in 1795. The varieties are few, and very distinct in appearance from other roses. The leaves are small, and of a deep shining green. This rose is not hardy, even in England; at least, the old varieties of it are not so: but one has lately been sent me, under the formidable appellation of ROSA BRACTEATA ALBA VENUSTA, which is reported to have proved hardy in New Jersey.

The Macartney roses are of a climbing habit, and evergreen.

ALBA ODORATA is white, with a yellow centre. The flowers are double. ALBA SIMPLEX is a single white. MARIA LEONIDA is white, with a blush centre, and is the best of the group. There is a hybrid rose raised by M. Hardy, of the Luxembourg Garden, and known by the name of BERBERIFOLIA HARDII. From its resemblance to this division, it is commonly placed with it, though not properly belonging here. It is a pretty rose, with bright yellow flowers, marked with a chocolate spot in the centre; but it is not hardy, nor is it easy of culture.

Rosa Lævigata. — No foreign work on the Rose includes this species among those held worthy of culture; yet in our Southern States, where it is naturalized, it is singularly beautiful. In the North it is not hardy, though the root commonly survives the winter, while the stem and branches are destroyed. It comes originally from China. Its shoots and leaves resemble those of the Banksia Rose; the former being long, pendulous, and graceful, and the latter of the most vivid green. Its flowers are single, very large, and of the purest waxy white, in the midst of which appears the bright yellow of the clustering stamens. Its long, slender, tapering buds are unsurpassed in beauty. It thrives admirably in a cool greenhouse, climbing with a rampant growth over the rafters, and giving forth a profusion of flowers through the greater part of the winter. Unlike all the other roses described in this book, it is a species in its original, undeveloped state, and, as such, offers a tempting subject for the art of the hybridist.

The Small Leafed Rose.

Rosa Microphylla.—This is an introduction within the present century from the Himalaya Mountains, and is rather a curiosity than an ornament. The leaves are very small and very numerous; and, by a curious freak of Nature, all the spines seem gathered together on the calyx, or outer covering of the flower-buds. The original variety, MICROPHYLLA RUBRA, is perhaps the best. Among others may be named CARNEA, COCCINEA, ROSEA, and PURPUREA.

There is a rose, commonly sold under the name of MICROPHYLLA RUGOSA, which is very desirable from the abundance of its autumnal bloom, and from its hardy nature; a point in which it differs from the true Microphyllas. It grows vigorously, and in autumn blooms profusely in large clusters of purplish-red flowers.

The Perpetual Moss Rose.
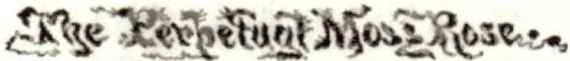

Rosa Centifolia.— This is a group of Moss roses to which, by hybridization, has been communicated some of the character of the autumn-blooming roses. The power of repeated blooming has, however, in some cases, been acquired at the expense of the distinctive characteristic of the Moss Rose; and few of this group are so well mossed as the parent to which they owe their name. One of the best is Salet, which is of a bright rose-color, tolerably well mossed, a vigorous grower, and an excellent autumn bloomer. Madame Edouard Ory is of a somewhat brighter hue, but by no means equal in vigor. The Perpetual White Moss is better deserving of the name of Moss than either of the others. It is double, blooms in clusters, and grows vigorously. Besides these, there are many other varieties, most of them indifferent.

These roses require the same culture with the Hybrid Perpetuals. Their power of autumnal blooming is increased by high enrichment and frequent transplanting.

The Perpetual Scotch Rose.

Rosa Spinosissima.—The Perpetual Scotch is a group of the well-known Scotch roses, endowed, probably by hybridization, with a power of blooming twice or more in the year. None of them are of much value except STANWELL, which is of a blush color, double, prettily cupped, and very fragrant.

Here closes our list of Autumnal roses, and with it our book. In conclusion, we would remind the cultivator, that although, even under neglect and scorn, the Rose has smiles for all, it is only to a loving and constant suitor that she clothes herself in all her beauty. Among all the flowers of our gardens, none is more grateful for a careful attention, and none more abundantly rewards it.

ROSES

MOST APPROVED BY THE BEST CULTIVATORS OF THE PRESENT DAY,

IN ADDITION TO

Those already mentioned under their respective Classes.

PROVENCE ROSES.

MADAME HENRIETTE, ROSY-PINK, VERY LARGE AND BEAUTIFUL.
MADAME L'ABBEY, BRIGHT ROSE, LARGE AND FULL.
ROYAL, PALE PINK, GLOBULAR AND LARGE, VERY FINE.
WHITE PROVENCE, PURE WHITE, LARGE AND FULL.

MOSS ROSES.

ADÈLE PAVIE, BLUSH.
ARISTIDES, BRIGHT CRIMSON.
ARTHUR YONG.
ÆTNA, BRILLIANT CRIMSON, TINTED WITH PURPLE.
FÉLICITÉ BOHAIN, BRIGHT ROSE, LARGE AND FULL.
GRACILIS, OR PROLIFIC, DEEP PINK, FREE BLOOMER, LARGE AND FULL.
HENRI MARTIN, SHADED VELVETY CARMINE, GOOD.
JAMES MITCHELL, ROSE-SHADED, FULL.
JOHN CRANSTON, CRIMSON-SHADED, FULL.
JULIE DE MERSENT, ROSE, SHADED WITH BLUSH.
LATONE, BLUSH, LARGE AND FULL.
MARIE DE BLOIS, ROSY-LILAC, LARGE AND FULL.

Madame de la Rochelambert, amaranth, large and full.
Pompon (Moss de Meaux), blush, peach centre, pretty, small and full.
Princess Alice, blush, pink centre.
Princesse Royale, salmon-flesh, full, fine form.
Princesse de Vaudemont, pink, good.
Purpurea Rubra, purple, large and full.
Reine Blanche, pure white, large and full.
Unique, pure white, large and full.
William Lobb, velvety-lake, very distinct.

DAMASK ROSES.

Calypso, shaded pink, large and good.
Columella, bright rose, large, full.
Helvetius, shaded rosy-crimson, very large and good.
Mariquita, white, lightly shaded, beautiful.

ALBA ROSES.

Blanchefleur, white.
Blush Hip, delicate blush, exquisite in bud, full.
Princesse Lamballe, white.

GALLICA ROSES

Aspasie, beautiful flesh, changing to blush, fine form.
Baron Cuvier, rosy-crimson, good shape.
Bizarre Marbrée, mottled crimson, large and very fine.
Colonel Coombes, light crimson, shaded with purple, very large and full.
Comte Plater, creamy-blush, splendid.
Comtesse de Segur, pale flesh, clear and beautiful, full, fine.
Docteur Deiltheim, rose, often shaded with purple, very large and full.
La Calaisienne, delicate pink, large and beautiful.
La Ville de Londres, shaded rose, very large and good.

LA VOLUPTÉ, OR LETITIA, BRIGHT ROSE, LARGE AND FULL.
LOUIS PHILIPPE, PINKISH-BLUSH, LIGHT MARGIN.
MADAME DUBERRY, MOTTLED CRIMSON-LAKE.
PRINCE REGENT, DEEP ROSE, SUPERB, LARGE AND FULL.
WILLIAM TELL, BRIGHT ROSE, EDGES BLUSH, VERY LARGE AND FULL.

HYBRID CHINA ROSES.

COMTE BOUBERT, LIGHT ROSE, LARGE AND VERY DOUBLE.
COMTESSE LACÉPÈDE, SILVERY-BLUSH, FLESH CENTRE, LARGE AND FULL.
COMTESSE MOLE, DELICATE ROSY-PINK, BEAUTIFUL.
ÉLISE MERCŒUR, PALE-SHADED ROSE, BEAUTIFUL.
FIMBRIATA, ROSY-CRIMSON, PETALS FRINGED AT EDGES.
FREDERICK THE SECOND, RICH CRIMSON-PURPLE, LARGE AND DOUBLE.
GENERAL ALLARD, FINE DEEP ROSE, VERY DOUBLE.
GÉNÉRAL LAMORICIÈRE, ROSE, FINE FORM, LARGE AND FULL, FINE.
GREAT WESTERN, BRIGHT REDDISH-CRIMSON, BEAUTIFUL.
JENNY, MOTTLED ROSY-PINK.
JUNO, PALE ROSE, BLUSH EDGES, VERY LARGE AND FULL.
LADY STUART, SILVERY-BLUSH, FINE FORM, MEDIUM AND FULL.
MADELINE (EMMELINE), PALE FLESH, EDGED WITH CRIMSON, BEAUTIFUL, LARGE, AND VERY DOUBLE.
NATHALIE DANIEL, PINK, FINE.
PERFECTION, DELICATE PINK, FINE FORM.
STADTHOLDER, SHADED PINK, VERY GOOD.
TRIOMPHE EN BEAUTÉ, DEEP-SHADED ROSE, GLOBULAR AND BEAUTIFUL.
TRIOMPHE DE LAQUEUE, PURPLISH-ROSE, LARGE AND SPLENDID.
WILLIAM JESSE, PURPLISH-CRIMSON, TINGED WITH LILAC, SUPERB, VERY LARGE AND VERY DOUBLE.

AUTUMNAL ROSES.

CHINA ROSES.

ABBÉ MIOLAND, FINE CRIMSON-RED, GOOD.
ANTHEROS, CREAMY-WHITE, LARGE AND FULL.

BELLE DE FLORENCE, LIGHT CARMINE, BLOOMS IN LARGE CLUSTERS.
ÉLISE FLEURY, FINE ROSE, LARGE AND FULL.
HENRY THE FIFTH, VIVID SCARLET, VERY GOOD.
LA FRAICHEUR, ROSY-WHITE, CENTRE YELLOWISH.
MADAME DESPREZ, WHITE, CENTRE LEMON.
MARJOLIN DE LUXEMBOURG, DARK CRIMSON, SUPERB, VERY LARGE AND FULL.
MIELLEZ, LEMON-WHITE, GOOD.
PRINCE CHARLES, BRIGHT CHERRY, VERY DOUBLE.
TANCREDE, FINE ROSY-PURPLE, DISTINCT, LARGE AND FULL.
VIRIDIFLORA, GREEN, CURIOUS.

TEA-SCENTED ROSES.

ABRICOTÉE, FAWN, APRICOT CENTRE, LARGE AND DOUBLE.
ADAM, BLUSH-ROSE, VERY SWEET, VERY LARGE AND FULL.
ALBA ROSA, WHITE, CENTRE ROSE, LARGE, FULL, AND VERY SWEET.
AMABILIS, FLESH-COLOR, LARGE AND FULL.
ARCHIMEDE, ROSY-FAWN, DARKER CENTRE, LARGE AND FULL.
AUGUSTE OGER, ROSE, CENTRE COPPER.
AUGUSTE VACHER, YELLOW, SHADED WITH COPPER-COLOR, LARGE AND FULL.
BELLE CHARTRONNAISE, RED, CHANGING TO CRIMSON, LARGE AND FULL.
BELLE DE BORDEAUX, PINK, LARGE AND FULL, HABIT AND GROWTH OF GLOIRE DE DIJON.
BRIDE OF ABYDOS, WHITE, SHADED WITH PINK, LARGE.
BURET, BRIGHT ROSY-PURPLE, DISTINCT, LARGE AND FULL.
CAROLINE, BLUSH-PINK, CENTRE DELICATE ROSE, LARGE AND FULL.
CLARA SYLVAIN, PURE WHITE, CENTRE CREAM, LARGE AND FULL.
CLIMBING DEVONIENSIS, IDENTICAL WITH THE OLD DEVONIENSIS IN FLOWER, BUT OF A RAPID RUNNING GROWTH, AND HENCE VALUABLE AS A CLIMBER.
COMTE DE PARIS, FLESH COLORED ROSE, SUPERB, VERY LARGE AND FULL.
COMTESSE DE BROSSARD, BRIGHT YELLOW, LARGE AND FULL.
COMTESSE DE LABARTHE, SALMON-PINK.
COMTESSE OUVAROFF, ROSE-SHADED, LARGE AND FULL.

DAVID PRADEL, ROSE, LARGE AND FULL.
DELPHINE GAUDOT, WHITE, LARGE AND DOUBLE.
DUC DE MAGENTA, SALMON, VERY LARGE AND FULL.
ÉLISE SAUVAGE, YELLOW, CENTRE ORANGE, BEAUTIFUL, LARGE AND FULL.
ENFANT DE LYON, PALE YELLOW, LARGE AND FULL.
EUGÈNE DESGACHES, CLEAR ROSE, BEAUTIFUL, LARGE AND FULL, VERY SWEET.
GENERAL TARTAS, DARK ROSE, LARGE AND FULL.
GERARD DESBOIS, BRIGHT RED, LARGE AND FULL, VERY SHOWY.
GLOIRE DE BORDEAUX, SILVERY-ROSE, THE BACK OF THE PETALS ROSY, VERY LARGE AND FULL.
GOUBAULT, BRIGHT ROSE, CENTRE BUFF, VERY LARGE AND DOUBLE.
GRANDIFLORA, SHADED ROSE, VERY LARGE AND DOUBLE.
HOMER, ROSE, CENTRE SALMON, VARIABLE, LARGE, FULL, AND GOOD.
JAUNE D'OR, FINE GOLDEN-YELLOW, OF MEDIUM SIZE, FULL, FORM GLOBULAR.
JAUNE OF SMITH (YELLOW NOISETTE), STRAW-COLOR, LARGE AND FULL.
JULIE MANSAIS, PURE WHITE, LARGE AND FULL.
LA BOULE D'OR, DEEP GOLDEN-YELLOW, LARGE AND FULL.
LAIS, PALE YELLOW, FULL, OF FINE FORM, BLOOMS FREELY.
L'ENFANT TROUVÉ, FINE, LARGE, PALE YELLOW.
LE PACTOLE, PALE YELLOW.
LOUISE DE SAVOIE, FINE YELLOW, LARGE AND FULL.
MADAME BLACHET, PALE ROSE, MEDIUM AND DOUBLE.
MADAME BRAVY, CREAMY-WHITE, LARGE AND FULL, PERFECT SHAPE.
MADAME CHARLES, SULPHUR-YELLOW, SALMON CENTRE, LARGE, FULL, AND OF GOOD FORM, FREE BLOOMER.
MADAME DE SERTOT, CREAM, GOOD.
MADAME DE ST. JOSEPH, SALMON-PINK, BEAUTIFUL, VERY LARGE AND DOUBLE, VERY SWEET.
MADAME DE TARTAS, BRIGHT ROSE, LARGE AND FULL, FREE BLOOMER.
MADAME DE VATRY, DEEP ROSE, LARGE AND FULL.
MADAME FALCOT, YELLOW, IN THE WAY OF SAFRANO, BUT OF A DEEPER SHADE, AND MORE DOUBLE.
MADAME HALPHIN, SALMON-PINK, CENTRE YELLOWISH, LARGE AND FULL.

Madame Laetay, yellow, shaded with salmon, large and full.
Madame Villermoz, white, centre salmon, large, full, and good.
Mademoiselle Adèle Jougant, clear yellow, medium size.
Madame Maurin, white, shaded with salmon, large and full.
Madame Pauline Labonté, salmon, large and full.
Maréchal Bugeaud, bright rose, large and full.
Maréchal Niel, beautiful deep yellow, large, full, and of globular form, very sweet, the shoots well clothed with large shining leaves.
Marquise de Foucault, white, fawn, and yellow, variable, large and double, one of the best.
Mirabile, pale yellow, edges dark rose, pretty, distinct.
Narcisse, fine pale yellow, large and full.
Nina, blush rose, fine, large and double.
Nisida, rose and yellow shaded, large and double.
Odorata, blush, centre rose, large and full.
President, rose, shaded with salmon, very large, and of good form.
Princess Adelaide, yellow, large and full.
Princesse Marie, rosy-pink, large and full, form globular.
Regulus, bright rose, shaded with copper, large and full.
Reine des Pays Bas, pale sulphur, free bloomer.
Rubens, white, shaded with rose, yellowish centre, large, full, and fine form.
Socrates, deep rose, centre apricot, large, full.
Sombreuil, white, tinged with rose, very large and full.
Souvenir de David, bright cherry-color, distinct and good.
Souvenir d'Élise Vardon, creamy-white, centre yellowish, very large and full; a splendid rose.
Souvenir de Mademoiselle Eugénie Pernet, white, tinged with flesh-color, and shaded with rose-salmon, large, full, and of good, hardy habit.
Triomphe de Guillot fils, white, shaded with rose and salmon, very large, full, and sweet; one of the best.
Triomphe du Luxembourg, coppery-rose, superb, very large and full.

VICOMTESSE DE CAZES, YELLOW, CENTRE DEEPER YELLOW, TINTED WITH COPPER-COLOR, LARGE AND VERY DOUBLE.
VICTORIA, YELLOW, CHANGING TO WHITE, LARGE AND FULL.

NOISETTE ROSES.

ADÈLE PAVIE, WHITE, ROSE CENTRE.
AIMÉE VIBERT SCANDENS, PURE WHITE, LARGE CLUSTERS.
BARONNE DE MAYNARD, FRENCH WHITE, BEAUTIFULLY CUPPED.
BLANCHE DE SOLVILLE, CREAMY-WHITE, TINGED PINK, STRONG GROWER.
CELINE FORESTIER, PALE YELLOW, FREE BLOOMER, LARGE AND FULL.
CERISE, ROSY-PURPLE, VERY GOOD.
CLAUDIE AUGUSTIN, WHITE, WITH YELLOWISH CENTRE.
CORNELIA KOCH, PALE YELLOW, VERY FULL AND FINE FORM.
DESPREZ À FLEUR JAUNE, RED, BUFF, AND SULPHUR, VARIABLE, VERY SWEET, LARGE AND FULL.
DU LUXEMBOURG, LILAC-ROSE, CENTRE DEEP RED, LARGE.
ÉCLAIR DE JUPITER, BRIGHT CRIMSON-SCARLET, LARGE AND DOUBLE.
EUPHROSINE, CREAMY-BUFF, VERY SWEET AND GOOD.
FELLENBERG, ROSY-CRIMSON, VERY FREE BLOOMER.
JANE HARDY, GOLDEN-YELLOW, LARGE AND FULL.
JACQUES ORMYOTT, DEEP ROSE, FINE.
LA BICHE, FLESH-WHITE, LARGE AND FULL.
LADY EMILY PEEL, SHADED FRENCH WHITE.
LAIS, FRENCH WHITE, LARGE AND GOOD.
MADAME DESLONGCHAMPS, CREAMY-WHITE, DEEPER CENTRE, BEAUTIFUL.
MADAME GUSTAVE BONNET, WHITE, TINGED WITH SALMON, FIRST CLASS.
MADAME SCHULTZ, PRIMROSE, SHADED WITH CARMINE, VERY SWEET.
MADEMOISELLE ARISTIDE, PALE YELLOW, CENTRE SALMON, LARGE AND FULL.
NARCISSE, FINE PALE YELLOW.
OCTAVIE, CRIMSON, LARGE, STRONG GROWER.
OPHIRIE, NANKEEN AND COPPER, DISTINCT, FULL.
PHALOË, ROSY-BUFF, VERY GOOD.
PUMILA ALBA, WHITE, SMALL AND DOUBLE.
TRIOMPHE DE LA DUCHERE, ROSY-BLUSH, LARGE AND FULL.
TRIOMPHE DE RENNES, CANARY, LARGE, FULL, AND FINE.
VICOMTESSE D'AVESNE, LIGHT SALMON-ROSE, LARGE, FULL, AND DISTINCT.

BOURBON ROSES.

APPOLINE, LIGHT PINK, LARGE AND FULL.
AURORE DU GUIDE, PURPLISH-VIOLET, SOMETIMES CRIMSON-SCARLET, LARGE AND FULL.
BARONNE DE NOIRMONT, PALE, SHADED ROSE, COMPACT AND GOOD.
BOUQUET DE FLORE, BRIGHT ROSY-CARMINE.
CATHERINE GUILLOT, BRIGHT ROSY-PINK, COMPACT, AND FIRST-RATE.
CELINE GONOD.
CHARLES ROBIN, FLESH-COLOR, SMALL, FULL, AND PRODUCED ABUNDANTLY.
COMICE DE TARNE ET GARONNE, CHERRY-COLOR.
COMTE DE MONTIJO, RICH REDDISH-PURPLE, VELVETY, FINE SHAPE.
COMTESSE DE BARBANTANNES, FLESH-COLOR, LARGE, FULL, AND OF FINE FORM.
DOCTEUR BERTHET, BRILLIANT CHERRY-RED, LARGE, FULL, AND GOOD.
DOCTEUR LEPRESTE, BRIGHT PURPLISH-RED, SHADED.
DUC DE CRILLON, BRILLIANT RED, CHANGING TO BRIGHT ROSE, LARGE AND FULL.
EDITH DE MURAT, FLESH-COLOR, CHANGING TO WHITE, OF FINE FORM.
EMOTION, DELICATE SHADED BLUSH, COMPACT AND GOOD.
EMPRESS EUGÉNIE, PALE ROSE, PURPLE EDGES, LARGE AND FULL, GOOD.
FERDINAND DIEPPE, REDDISH-VIOLET, BRIGHT AND GOOD.
GEORGE CUVIER, BRIGHT ROSE, FINE FORM, LARGE AND FULL.
GLOIRE DE ROSOMÈNES, BRIGHT CRIMSON, SEMI-DOUBLE, BUT EFFECTIVE.
GLORIETTA, DEEP RED, OR CRIMSON.
GOURDAULT, RICH PURPLE, FINE FORM, FULL.
JOSEPHINE CLERMONT, PINK, FULL.
JULIE DE FONTENELLE, CRIMSON-PURPLE, FINE FORM, FULL.
JUSTINE, ROSY-CARMINE, GOOD, VERY DOUBLE.
L'AVENIR, BRIGHT ROSE, LARGE, FULL, AND OF GOOD FORM.
LA QUINTINIE, BRIGHT CRIMSON, SHADED, OR CHANGING TO BLACKISH-VIOLET, FULL.
LE FLORIFÈRE, ROSE, WITH A LILAC AND CRIMSON TINT, LARGE AND FULL.
LEON OURSEL, LIGHT RED, LARGE, FULL, AND GOOD.
LOUISE MARGOTTIN, BEAUTIFUL BRIGHT ROSY-PINK, CUPPED AND GOOD.

LIST OF ROSES.

Madame Angelina, rich cream, fawn centre, medium size, distinct.
Madame Cousin, flesh-colored rose, large and full.
Madame de Stella, delicate pink, very double, fine shape, first class.
Madame Desprez, lilac-rose, large and full.
Madame Élise de Chenier, bright rose, blooms freely.
Madame Helfenbein, pale rose, very good.
Madame Josephine Guyet, deep red.
Madame La Comtesse, bright pink, fine shape.
Madame Manoel, light-shaded pink, very large.
Madame Maréchal, flesh, white edges, distinct and good.
Madame Nerard, silvery-blush, centre pink.
Mademoiselle C. Riguet, pure white, very abundant bloomer.
Mademoiselle Félicité Truillot, bright rose, abundant bloomer.
Marguerite Bonnet, fleshy-white, large and good.
Marquis Balbiano, rose, tinged with silver, full, fine form, distinct.
Marquis d'Ivry, lilac-rose, forms a large and showy head.
Marquis de Moyra, rose, shaded with vermilion, fine form, large.
Marquis de Murat, pink, pale edges.
Menoux, bright red, approaching to scarlet, full.
Michel Bonnet, bright rosy-pink, fine.
Modèle de Perfection, delicate pink, compact, and most beautiful.
Monsieur Jard, cherry-red, large and full.
Octavie Fontaine, white, tinted with flesh-color, good shape.
Omar Pacha, brilliant red, large, full, and good form.
Phénix, purplish-red, large and fine.
Pierre de St. Cyr, pink, large and full.
Prince de Chimay, purplish-crimson, large and fine, flowers freely.
Queen, buff-rose, free bloomer, large and double.
Reine de Castille, light rose, good.
Rev. H. Dombrain, brilliant carmine, fine shape.
Reveil, cherry, richly shaded with violet.
Souchet, deep crimson-purple, vivid, superb.

SOUVENIR DE LOUIS GAUDIN, REDDISH-PURPLE, SHADED WITH BLACK, FINE FORM, FULL, ABUNDANT BLOOMER.

VICOMTE DE CUSSY, LIVELY RED, LARGE, AND VERY DOUBLE.

VICTOR EMANUEL, PURPLE AND PURPLISH-MAROON, LARGE AND DOUBLE, GOOD AND DISTINCT.

HYBRID PERPETUAL ROSES.

ABBÉ REYNAUD, CLEAR DARK VIOLET, LARGE, FULL, DISTINCT, AND FINE; GOOD HABIT.

ABD-EL-KADER, DEEP VELVETY-CRIMSON, GOOD.

ADMIRAL NELSON, CRIMSON, COLOR BEAUTIFUL.

ADOLPHE NOBLET, ROSY-CARMINE, VERY BEAUTIFUL.

AGATOIDE, LIVELY ROSE, SHADED WITH DEEP ROSE, FULL.

ALCIDE VIGNERON, BRIGHT ROSE, LARGE AND FULL.

ALEXANDRE DUMAS, VELVETY-MAROON, HIGHLY SCENTED.

ALEXANDRE FONTAINE, REDDISH-CERISE, FINE FORM.

ALEXANDRINE BACHMETEFF, BRIGHT RED, LARGE, FULL, AND SHOWY.

ALEXANDRINE BELFROY, PEACH-COLOR, LARGE AND FULL.

ALFRED DE ROUGEMONT, CRIMSON-PURPLE, SHADED WITH FIERY RED, VERY BRIGHT, LARGE AND FULL.

ALPAIDE DE ROTALIER, FINE TRANSPARENT ROSE-COLOR, GLOSSY, LARGE, FULL, AND OF GOOD FORM.

ALPHONSE BELIN, CLEAR BRILLIANT RED, THE REVERSE OF THE PETALS WHITISH, LARGE, FULL, AND OF FINE FORM.

ALPHONSE DAMAIZIN, BRILLIANT-SHADED CRIMSON, GOOD FORM AND HABIT.

ALPHONSE DE LAMARTINE, LIGHT ROSY-PINK.

ALPHONSE KARR, BRIGHT ROSE, FULL.

AMIRAL GRAVINA, BLACKISH-PURPLE, CHANGING TO AMARANTH, LARGE AND FULL.

AMIRAL LA PEYROUSE, BRILLIANT CRIMSON, SOMETIMES DARK CRIMSON, SHADED WITH VIOLET, LARGE, FULL, AND VERY FINE.

ANDRÉ LEROY, PURPLISH-CRIMSON, FINE COLOR, LARGE AND FULL.

ANNA ALEXIEFF, PRETTY ROSE-COLOR, LARGE, FULL, AND OF GOOD HABIT; FLOWERS FREELY.

ANNA DE DIESBACH, CLEAR ROSE, FINE COLOR, VERY LARGE AND SHOWY.

LIST OF ROSES.

ARCHEVÊQUE DE PARIS, SHADED VELVETY-MAROON.
ARLES DUFOUR, DEEP PURPLE, WITH VIOLET CENTRE, LARGE, AND DEEP IMBRICATED FORM, BEAUTIFUL NEW ROSE.
ARMIDE, ROSY-SALMON, DISTINCT, IMBRICATED, AND FULL FORM.
AUGUSTE GUINOISSEAU, SHADED DARK CRIMSON, VERY LARGE.
AURORE, SALMON-ROSE, LARGE AND FULL, DISTINCT.
BARLOW, BRIGHT ROSY-CRIMSON.
BARON ADOLPHE DE ROTHSCHILD, FIERY RED, PETALS OFTEN EDGED WITH WHITE, LARGE, FULL, AND VERY EFFECTIVE.
BARON GONELLA, PINK AND LILAC SHADED, LARGE, FULL, AND FINE.
BARONNE DAUMESNIL, BEAUTIFUL BRIGHT ROSE, LARGE, FULL, AND OF GOOD FORM.
BARONNE DE HECKEREN, ROSY-PINK, VERY LARGE AND DOUBLE.
BARONNE HALLEZ, DARK RED, FULL, AND OF FINE FORM.
BARONNE NOIRMONT, DEEP ROSE, LARGE, AND OF GOOD FORM.
BARONNE PELLETAN DE KINKELIN, CRIMSON AND PURPLE SHADED, COLORS BRILLIANT, LARGE, FULL, AND OF FINE FORM.
BEAUTÉ FRANÇAISE, VELVETY VIOLET-RED, REVERSE OF PETALS FIERY RED, LARGE, FULL, AND WELL FORMED.
BELLE ANGLAISE, BEAUTIFUL BRIGHT PINK, FINE SHAPE.
BELLE DE BOURG LA REINE, SATIN-ROSE, LARGE AND FULL, FINE FORM.
BELLE DES MASSIFS, BEAUTIFUL ROSY-PINK.
BELLE DU PRINTEMPS, BEAUTIFUL PALE, MOTTLED ROSE.
BERCEAU IMPÉRIAL, FLESH-COLOR, LARGE AND FULL.
BERNARD PALISSY, BRIGHT CARMINE, LARGE, FULL, AND VERY FINE; GOOD HABIT.
BUFFON, LIGHT ROSY-CRIMSON.
BURKE, ROSY-LILAC, OR VIOLET, FULL.
CATHERINE GUILLOT, DEEP PINK, PERFECT FORM; ONE OF THE BEST.
CENTIFOLIA ROSEA, BRIGHT PINK, LARGE, OF BEAUTIFUL CUPPED FORM.
CHRISTIAN PUTTNER, PURPLE, SHADED WITH CRIMSON, LARGE AND FULL.
CLAUDE MILLION, SCARLET-CRIMSON, DASHED WITH ROSE AND VIOLET, VELVETY, LARGE, FULL, AND OF EXCELLENT FORM, HABIT GOOD.
CLEMENT MAROT, CLEAR ROSY-LILAC, LARGE AND VERY DOUBLE.
CLEOSTINE, LARGE ROSE, LARGE, FINE GLOBULAR FORM.
COLONEL DE ROUGEMONT, PALE ROSE, SHADED WITH CARMINE, VERY LARGE AND FULL.

Colonel Soufflot, beautiful rosy-pink.
Comte Cavour, pale-shaded rose, fine.
Comte de Nanteuil, bright rose, darker edges, large and full.
Comtesse Barbantanne, flesh-color, large, full, and of fine form, free and good.
Comtesse de Courcy, rose, shaded with brilliant red, flowers very freely.
Comtesse de Kergorlay, bright glossy purple, large and full.
Comtesse de Séguier, velvety-red, shaded with violet, large and full.
Darzens, salmon-rose, large and double, very sweet.
Deuil de Prince Albert, blackish-crimson, shaded, centre fiery red, large, full, and good.
Dominique Daran, dark crimson-purple, large and very double.
Dr. Juillard, rosy-purple, shaded with carmine, large and double.
Dr. Spitzer, bright red, large, fine globular form.
Duc d'Anjou, crimson, shaded with dark red, very large, full, and well formed.
Duc de Bassano, dark velvety-crimson, cupped, large and full; one of the best.
Duc d'Harcourt, bright reddish-carmine, blooming freely and in clusters, large and full.
Duc de Ruschpler, deep rose, full.
Duc d'Ossuna, rich crimson.
Duchesse de Magenta, flesh, changing to white, distinct and beautiful.
Duchesse d'Orléans, fine lavender-blush, large, full, and good.
Duchess of Norfolk, rich purple-crimson, medium, double.
Duchess of Sutherland, pale rose, large, and very double.
Duke of Cambridge, cherry-red, fine form.
Éclair de Jupiter, rosy-crimson, large and showy.
Émile Dulac, bright rose, large, full, and deeply cupped; the best of the color.
Emotion, white, tinted with rose, of medium size, full, form perfect, flowers abundantly.
Eugène Appert, scarlet and crimson shaded, splendid colors, fine foliage, free bloomer.

EUGÈNE BOURCIER, PURPLE-REDDISH, VELVETY, LARGE AND FULL.

EUGÈNE VERDIER, RICH DARK VIOLET, LARGE, FULL, AND OF PERFECT FORM; ONE OF THE BEST.

EUGÉNIE LEBRUN, DARK CRIMSON, LARGE AND FULL.

ÉVÊQUE DE NISMES, SCARLET AND CRIMSON, FULL, FLAT FORM.

FERNANDO, FIERY RED, TINTED WITH WHITE, LARGE, FULL, AND VERY SWEET.

FRANÇOIS LACHARME, BRIGHT CARMINE, CHANGING TO RED, FULL AND GLOBULAR; A SUPERB ROSE.

FRANÇOIS LOUVAT, LILAC-RED, LARGE, FULL, GLOBULAR, GOOD, AND DISTINCT.

FRANÇOIS PREMIER, CHERRY-RED, SHADED, FINE FORM.

GABRIEL DE PEYRONNEY, FIERY RED, SHADED WITH VIOLET TOWARDS THE CENTRE, LARGE, FULL, AND OF FINE FORM.

GÉNÉRAL CASTELLANE, BRIGHT CRIMSON, LARGE AND FULL.

GENERAL SIMPSON, BRIGHT CARMINE, FULL AND FREE.

GEORGE PAUL, BRIGHT RED, VELVETY, BLOOMING IN CLUSTERS, LARGE AND FULL.

GEORGE PRINCE, FINE BRILLIANT RED, SHADED WITH DARK ROSE, REVERSE OF PETALS WHITISH, LARGE, FULL, FORM GLOBULAR.

GLOIRE DE CHATILLON, BRILLIANT RED, SHADED WITH VIOLET, LARGE AND FULL.

GLOIRE DE VITRY, BRIGHT ROSE, LARGE AND FULL.

GLOIRE DU SACRÉ CŒUR, FLESH-COLORED ROSE, TIPPED WITH BRIGHT RED, AND SHADED WITH PURPLE; GOOD HABIT.

GUSTAVE CORAUX, BRIGHT PURPLE, FREE IN AUTUMN.

GUSTAVE ROUSSEAU, PURPLE, SHADED WITH VIOLET-RED, LARGE, AND FULL.

HENRI IV., SHADED VERMILION, VERY GOOD.

HÉROINE VAUCLUSE, CLEAR ROSE, BEAUTIFUL FORM, FREE BLOOMER.

H. LAURENTIUS, FINE REDDISH-CRIMSON, SHADED WITH BLACK, VELVETY, LARGE, AND FULL; FORM CUPPED.

HORTENSE BLACHETTE, WHITE, WITH ROSY CENTRE, MEDIUM SIZE, FULL.

IMPÉRATRICE EUGÉNIE, WHITE, TINTED WITH ROSE, FULL AND GOOD.

IMPÉRATRICE MARIA ALEXANDRINA, WHITE, TINGED WITH BLUSH, GOOD FORM, MEDIUM SIZE, FULL.

JAMES DICKSON, VELVETY-LAKE, SEMI-DOUBLE.

JEAN-BAPTISTE GUILLOT, VELVETY-CARMINE.
JEAN BART, RED AND VIOLET SHADED, BRILLIANT, VERY EFFECTIVE.
JEAN GOUJON, BEAUTIFUL CLEAR RED, VERY LARGE, FULL, AND GOOD.
JEAN TOUVAIS, BEAUTIFUL REDDISH-PURPLE, SHADED WITH CRIMSON, VERY LARGE, FULL, AND OF EXCELLENT FORM; BLOOMS FREELY.
JOHN HOPPER, ROSE, CRIMSON CENTRE, REVERSE OF THE PETALS PURPLISH-LILAC, LARGE AND FULL.
JOHN STANDISH, VERY DARK CRIMSON, FINE GLOBULAR FORM.
JOSEPH FIALA, BRIGHT DARK-RED, WITH WHITISH EDGING, LARGE AND FULL, FORM CUPPED.
KATE HAUSBURG, FINE BRIGHT ROSE, LARGE, FULL, AND OF EXCELLENT SHAPE AND SUBSTANCE.
L'ABBÉ LAURY, BRIGHT RED.
L'AVENIR, GLOSSY PINK, LARGE, FULL, AND OF GOOD FORM.
LA BRILLANTE, TRANSPARENT CARMINE, VERY BRIGHT AND BEAUTIFUL, LARGE, AND OF FINE FORM.
LA DUCHESSE DE MORNY, BRIGHT BUT DELICATE ROSE-COLOR, THE REVERSE OF THE PETALS SILVERY, LARGE AND FULL, FORM GLOBULAR.
L'ÉBLOUISSANTE, BRILLIANT RED, LARGE, FULL, AND OF GOOD HABIT.
L'ÉCLATANTE, BRIGHT RED, CHANGING TO VIOLET-RED, LARGE, FULL, AND OF GOOD FORM.
L'ÉLÉGANTE, BLUSH-WHITE, FULL, FREE, FLAT FORM.
LÆLIA, SHADED ROSE, VERY LARGE, FULL, AND VERY FINE.
LA ESMERALDA, BRIGHT CHERRY-COLOR, LARGE, FULL, AND OF GOOD FORM.
LAFONTAINE, PURPLISH-ROSE, VERY LARGE AND FULL.
LA PHOCÉENNE, BLACKISH-CRIMSON, FINE SHELL-SHAPED, CUPPED FORM.
LA PIVOINE, SHADED ROSY-CARMINE, PECULIAR FOLIAGE.
LA REINE DE LA PAPE, FINE ROSY-PINK, LARGE AND BEAUTIFUL.
LA TOUR DE COURCY, ROSY-PINK, VERY GOOD.
LAURENT DESCOURT, DEEP PURPLISH-CRIMSON, RICH AND VELVETY, LARGE AND FULL.
LA VILLE DE ST. DENIS, ROSY-CARMINE, FINE FORM, LARGE AND FULL.
LE BARON DE ROTHSCHILD, DARK REDDISH-CARMINE, SOMETIMES SHADED WITH VIOLET, VERY LARGE AND FULL.
LE GÉANT, CLEAR BRIGHT ROSE, TINTED WITH VIOLET, VERY LARGE AND FULL, BLOOMS FREELY; THE LARGEST ROSE YET INTRODUCED.

LE MONT D'OR, PALE ROSE, CUPPED AND DOUBLE.

LÉOPOLD HAUSBURG, BRIGHT CARMINE, SHADED WITH PURPLE, LARGE AND DOUBLE, OF FINE FORM.

LÉOPOLD PREMIER, BRIGHT DARK-RED, VERY LARGE AND FULL, FINE FORM.

LÉON DES COMBATS, REDDISH-VIOLET, OFTEN SHADED WITH SCARLET, LARGE AND FULL.

LORD CLYDE, CRIMSON AND PURPLE, DEEPLY SHADED, LARGE AND FULL.

LORD HERBERT, ROSY-CARMINE, THE PETALS REFLEXING AT THE SUMMITS; LARGE, FULL, FINELY FORMED.

LORD PALMERSTON, CHERRY-RED, FULL, FINE FORM; FLOWERS FREELY.

LOUIS VAN HOUTTE, BRIGHT ROSY-CARMINE, VERY LARGE, FULL, AND OF FINE, GLOBULAR FORM.

LOUIS XIV., RICH BLOOD-COLOR, LARGE AND FULL, FORM GLOBULAR; A DISTINCT AND BEAUTIFUL VARIETY.

LOUISE DAMAIZIN, WHITE, WITH PEACH CENTRE, GOOD SIZE AND FORM.

LOUISE DARZENS, PURE WHITE, NOT LARGE, BUT FULL, AND OF FINE FORM; ONE OF THE BEST FOR MASSING.

LOUISE D'AUTRICHE, ROSE, LARGE AND FULL.

LOUISE GULINO, VELVETY-MAROON, FINE.

LOUISE ODIER, FINE BRIGHT ROSE, FULL, VERY FREE BLOOMER.

MADAME ALFRED DE ROUGEMONT, PURE WHITE, LIGHTLY AND DELICATELY SHADED WITH ROSE AND CARMINE, LARGE AND FULL, SHAPE OF THE CABBAGE ROSE; ONE OF THE BEST.

MADAME VAN GEERT, ROSY-PINK, STRIPED WHITE, VERY BEAUTIFUL.

MADAME BOUTIN, CHERRY-CRIMSON, LARGE AND FULL.

MADAME BRIANSON, REDDISH-CARMINE, SHADED WITH LIGHT RED, VERY LARGE AND FULL.

MADAME BRUNI, DELICATE PEACH, LARGE AND FULL.

MADAME CAILLAT, BRIGHT CERISE, LARGE, FULL, AND OF GOOD HABIT.

MADAME C. CRAPELET, ROSY-RED, LARGE, FULL, AND VERY FINE.

MADAME CELINE TOUVAIS, SHADED CARMINE.

MADAME CHARLES ROY, SHADED ROSY-CRIMSON, GOOD SHAPE.

MADAME CHARLES WOOD, VINOUS-CRIMSON, VERY LARGE, FULL, AND EFFECTIVE.

MADAME CRESPIN, ROSE, SHADED WITH DARK VIOLET, MEDIUM SIZE, FULL, FORM GOOD.

MADAME DE CAMBACÈBES, ROSY-CARMINE, LARGE AND FULL, FINE FORM.
MADAME DE CANROBERT, WHITE, SLIGHTLY TINGED WITH PEACH, LARGE AND FULL, NICELY CUPPED.
MADAME DERREUX DOUVILLE, DELICATE GLOSSY ROSE, BORDERED WITH WHITE, LARGE, FULL, AND OF FINE FORM; GOOD HABIT.
MADAME DE STELLA, BRIGHT ROSE, LARGE, FULL, AND OF FINE FORM.
MADAME DOMAGE, BRIGHT ROSE, VERY LARGE AND DOUBLE.
MADAME DUCHÈRE, ROSY-WHITE, DELICATE TINT, FULL.
MADAME EMAIN, FINE PURPLISH-RED, GLOBULAR, LARGE AND FULL.
MADAME ERNEST DRÉOL, DARK ROSE, SHADED WITH LILAC, LARGE, FULL, AND OF GOOD FORM, FOLIAGE FINE.
MADAME EUGÈNE VERDIER, DEEP PINK, LARGE, FULL, AND FINELY CUPPED.
MADAME FREEMAN, CREAMY-WHITE, MEDIUM SIZE, GLOBULAR AND FULL, THOROUGHLY PERPETUAL.
MADAME HECTOR JACQUIN, CLEAR ROSE, SHADED WITH LILAC, LARGE AND FULL.
MADAME HELYE, CARMINE, SHADED-LILAC, MEDIUM, DISTINCT.
MADAME JULIE DARAN, PURPLISH-VERMILION, GLOSSY, VERY LARGE AND FULL; ONE OF THE BEST.
MADAME LAFFAY, ROSY-CRIMSON, LARGE AND DOUBLE.
MADAME LOUISE CARIQUE, FINE ROSE AND CARMINE, FULL.
MADAME MASSON, REDDISH-CRIMSON, CHANGING TO VIOLET, VELVETY, LARGE AND FULL.
MADAME MELAINE, SHADED VERMILION.
MADAME PAULINE VILLOT, CRIMSON-PURPLE, FINE FORM; BLOOMS FREELY.
MADAME PHELIP, SILVERY-ROSE, BEAUTIFULLY SHADED WITH CRIMSON, SMALL AND PRETTY.
MADAME PIERSON, BRIGHT RED, SILVERY EDGES, LARGE AND GLOBULAR.
MADAME PLACE, BEAUTIFUL LIGHT ROSE, SMALL, BUT PRETTY FORM.
MADAME SCHMIDT, SHADED ROSY-PINK, LARGE AND BEAUTIFUL.
MADAME SOUPPERT, BEAUTIFUL PALE FLESH-COLOR, FINE FORM.
MADAME STANDISH, CLEAR PALE PINK, DELICATE COLOR, LARGE AND FULL.

Madame Sylvain Caubert, bright rose, delicately edged with white; very distinct.

Madame Thérèse Levet, pale pink, globular and good.

Madame Valembourg, bright purplish-red, shaded, large, full, and of good form.

Madame Victor Verdier, rich bright rosy-cherry color, large, full, and fine formed, cupped; blooms in clusters.

Madame Vigneron, pale rose, large and full, very sweet and good.

Mademoiselle Alice Leroy, delicate rose, shaded, fine form, full.

Mademoiselle Betsy Hainman, brilliant cerise; a most effective climber.

Mademoiselle Bonnaire, white, rosy-centre, large, full, and of exquisite form; one of the best.

Mademoiselle Emain, white, rosy centre, full, and of good form.

Mademoiselle Gabrielle de Peyronney, bright red, with shaded centre, large, full.

Mademoiselle Goddard, rosy-pink, light margin, good.

Thérèse Appert, peach-color, large and full, cupped, good shape, free bloomer.

Maréchal Canrobert, fine bright rose, sometimes shaded with purple, very large, habit good.

Maréchal Forey, velvety-crimson, reverse of petals violet, large and full.

Maréchal Souchet, beautiful reddish-crimson, shaded with dark maroon, very large and full, petals also large, habit good; one of the best.

Maréchal Souchet (Damaizin), fine rosy-carmine, large, full, and of exquisite form.

Maréchal Vaillant, purplish-red, very large, full, and of good form.

Marguerite Appert, lavender-blush, large and full, form cupped, pretty and distinct.

Marie Portemer, purplish-red, full, and fine form.

Mathurin Regnier, beautiful pale rose, large and full.

Maxime, violet-rose, large and full.

MEXICO, VELVETY REDDISH-PURPLE, SHADED WITH BLACKISH-VIOLET, LARGE AND FULL, BLOOMS FREELY, HABIT GOOD.
MODÈLE DE PERFECTION, LIVELY PINK, VERY PRETTY, BLOOMS FREELY; ONE OF THE BEST.
MONSIEUR DE MONTIGNY, ROSY-CARMINE, LARGE AND FULL.
MONSIEUR JOIGNEAUX, SHADED MAROON, STRONG GROWER.
MONSIEUR MOREAU, SHADED CRIMSON.
MONTE CHRISTO, BLACKISH-PURPLE, OFTEN DASHED WITH SCARLET, VERY RICH COLOR, LARGE AND GOOD IN FORM.
MRS. CHARLES WOOD, BRIGHT RED, LARGE, FULL, AND SUPERB FORM.
MRS. ELLIOT, PURPLE, LARGE AND DOUBLE.
MURILLO, RICH PURPLISH-RED, SHADED WITH CARMINE AND VIOLET, LARGE, DOUBLE, AND OF GOOD FORM.
NOEMI, BLUSH, PINK CENTRE, FULL.
NOTRE DAME DE FOURVIÈRES, PALE SATIN-ROSE, LARGE AND FULL.
ODERIC VITAL, SILVERY-ROSE, LARGE AND FULL, GOOD FORM.
OLIVIER DELHOMME, BRILLIANT PURPLISH-RED, LARGE, AND PERFECT SHAPE, FOLIAGE HANDSOME.
PANACHÉE D'ORLÉANS, FLESH, STRIPED WITH ROSE AND PURPLE, DISTINCT.
PARMENTIER, ROSY-PINK, BLOOMS FREELY, VERY BRILLIANT.
PAUL DE LA MEILLERAY, FINE PURPLISH-CERISE, VERY LARGE, FULL, AND OF EXCELLENT FORM.
PAUL DESGRAND, FINE BRIGHT-RED, LARGE AND FULL, FORM GLOBULAR.
PAUL DUPUY, VELVETY-CRIMSON, SHADED, LARGE AND FULL.
PAUL FEVAL, CHERRY-COLOR, LARGE AND FULL, FORM CUPPED.
PAULINE LANSÉZEUR, BRIGHT CRIMSON, CHANGING TO VIOLET, FULL.
PAULINE VILLOT, SHADED ROSY-CARMINE, COMPACT AND GOOD.
PAVILLON DE PREGNY, WHITE AND RED, MEDIUM SIZE, FULL, MOST ABUNDANT BLOOMER.
PETER LAWSON, BRILLIANT RED, SHADED WITH CARMINE, LARGE AND DOUBLE.
PIERRE NOTTING, BLACKISH-RED, SHADED WITH VIOLET, VERY LARGE AND FULL, FORM GLOBULAR, HABIT GOOD; ONE OF THE BEST.
PRAIRIE DE TERRE NOIRE, VELVETY-PURPLE, LARGE AND FULL.
PRINCE HENRI DES PAYS BAS, BRIGHT CRIMSON, SHADED WITH VELVETY-PURPLE, OF MEDIUM SIZE, FULL, FINE.

PRINCE IMPÉRIAL, ROSY-CARMINE, LARGE AND FULL.
PRINCE LEON, FINE BRIGHT CRIMSON, LARGE, AND VERY DOUBLE.
PRINCE NOIR, VERY DARK MAROON, GOOD CLIMBER.
PRINCESS ALICE, BRIGHT ROSE, THE REVERSE OF THE PETALS WHITISH, LARGE, FULL, AND SWEET; A DISTINCT AND DESIRABLE VARIETY.
PRINCESSE IMPÉRIALE CLOTILDE, GLOSSY-WHITE, PINK CENTRE.
PRINCESSE MATHILDE, CRIMSON, MAROON, AND PURPLE SHADED, COLORS EXQUISITE, MEDIUM SIZE, DOUBLE, FORM EXPANDED; A GOOD HARDY VARIETY.
PROFESSOR KOCH, BRIGHT ROSY-CERISE, SHADED WITH CARMINE, BEAUTIFULLY CUPPED; ONE OF THE BEST.
QUEEN, ROSE, VERY LARGE AND BEAUTIFUL.
RED ROVER, FIERY RED, GROWTH MORE THAN USUALLY VIGOROUS, FLOWERING UP TO CHRISTMAS. NOT DOUBLE ENOUGH FOR A SHOW ROSE, BUT THE FINEST AND MOST EFFECTIVE OF PILLAR ROSES.
REINE DE CASTILLE, WHITISH-ROSE, LARGE AND FULL, OF GOOD HABIT, AND BLOOMS FREELY.
REINE DE LA CITÉ, BLUSH, PINK CENTRE, LARGE, FULL, AND OF GOOD HABIT.
REYNOLDS HOLE, LIVELY PINK, INCREASING IN BRILLIANCY AS THE FLOWERS ADVANCE IN AGE, LARGE, NOT VERY FULL.
RICHARD SMITH, VELVETY-MAROON, VERY DARK.
ROBERT FORTUNE, BRIGHT RED, LARGE, FULL, AND GOOD.
SENATEUR REVEIL, BRILLIANT REDDISH-CRIMSON, SHADED WITH DARK PURPLE, LARGE AND FULL, FORM FINE, BLOOMS FREELY, HABIT GOOD.
SIMON OPPENHEIM, MAROON, SHADED VERMILION, VERY FINE.
SOUVENIR DE BÉRANGER, LIGHT ROSE, VERY LARGE AND DOUBLE.
SOUVENIR DE CHARLES MONTAULT, BRILLIANT RED, CUPPED, LARGE AND FULL, FREE BLOOMER.
SOUVENIR DE COMTE CAVOUR, CRIMSON AND BLACK SHADED, OF GOOD SIZE AND FORM.
SOUVENIR DE LADY EARDLEY, REDDISH-SCARLET, RICHLY SHADED, LARGE, VERY LIGHT, AND EFFECTIVE.
SOUVENIR DE LEVESON GOWER, FINE DARK RED, CHANGING TO RUBY, VERY LARGE AND FULL.

Souvenir de M. Rousseau, scarlet, changing to crimson, shaded with maroon, very rich and velvety, large and very double.
Toujours Fleuri, violet-purple, full and good.
Triomphe d'Alençon, bright red, very large, full, and fine.
Triomphe d'Amiens, vivid crimson, sometimes striped with lake, large and double.
Triomphe d'Angers, crimson-scarlet, large, full, free.
Triomphe de Bagatelle, bright cherry-carmine, large, full, and free.
Triomphe de Caen, deep velvety-purple, shaded with scarlet-crimson, large and full.
Triomphe de Lyon, shaded maroon, beautiful.
Triomphe de Villecresnes, clear red, more brilliant at the centre, large and full, blooms freely.
Turenne, brilliant red, large, handsome petals, very effective.
Vainqueur de Goliath, brilliant-crimson-scarlet, very large and double.
Vainqueur de Solferino, dark red, brighter centre, large, full, blooms abundantly.
Vase d'Élection, bright rose.
Veloutée d'Orléans, brilliant velvety-red, almost scarlet, large and full.
Vicomte Vigier, bright violet-red, large, full, and good.
Vicomtesse Belleval, beautiful blush, large and full, fine form, blooms freely, habit good.
Vicomtesse de Montesquieu, double white, useful as a bedder.
Vicomtesse Douglas, beautiful rose, the reverse of the petals whitish, very large and full, form cupped.
Victor Trouillard, brilliant crimson and purple shaded, large and full.
Vulcan, bright purplish-violet, shaded with black, good and distinct.
Wilhelm Pfitzer, brilliant red, color often superb, large and full.
William Jesse, crimson, tinged with lilac, superb, very large and double.

WILLIAM PAUL, BRILLIANT REDDISH-CRIMSON, LARGE AND FULL; A FREE, HARDY, LATE-BLOOMING ROSE, EXCELLENT FOR BEDDING.

PERPETUAL MOSS ROSES.

ALFRED DE DALMAS, ROSE, EDGES ROSY-WHITE, BLOOMING IN CLUSTERS, FULL.

EUGÈNE DE SAVOIE, BRIGHT RED, LARGE AND FULL.

EUGÉNIE GUINOISEAU, BRIGHT CHERRY, CHANGING TO VIOLET, LARGE, FULL, AND WELL MOSSED.

HORTENSE VERNET, WHITE, TINGED WITH LIGHT ROSE, FINE, LARGE, AND FULL.

JAMES VEITCH, DEEP VIOLET, SHADED WITH CRIMSON, LARGE AND DOUBLE.

MADAME LA RIVIÈRE, ROSY-PINK, DISTINCT AND GOOD.

POMPONE, MOTTLED ROSE, ABUNDANT BLOOMER.

RAPHAEL, FLESH-COLOR, FLOWERING IN CORYMBS, LARGE, FULL.

NEW ROSES OF 1866.

The following are the most promising of the latest new roses. The descriptions are those of the raisers; and as the varieties have not yet bloomed in this country, and very few of them in England, it is impossible to speak of them definitely. Most of them are results of the skill and perseverance of French cultivators.

The letters immediately succeeding the name refer to the class,— H. P., Hybrid Perpetual; B., Bourbon; T., Tea-scented.

ABBÉ BERLÈZE, H. P.; flowers varying from bright-reddish cerise to rosy-carmine, large, full, and of fine form; growth vigorous.

ACHILLE GONOD, H. P.; flowers bright-reddish carmine; a seedling from *Jules Margottin*; very large and full; extra fine foliage, dark green; growth vigorous.

ADRIENNE DE CARDOVILLE, B.; flowers delicate rose, of medium size; full, perfect form.

AUGUSTE RIVIÈRE, H. P.; flowers beautiful bright-reddish carmine, the reverse of the petals of a paler hue, distinctly edged with white; large, and of regular globular form; growth vigorous.

BAPTISTE DESPORTES, H. P.; flowers bright scarlet, very abundant, of medium size, full; growth vigorous.

BARONNE DE MAYNARD, B.; flowers beautiful pure white, of medium size, fine form; growth vigorous.

BEAUTY OF WESTERHAM, H. P. (*Cattell*); flowers brilliant scarlet; foliage bright green; habit free and vigorous; fragrance powerful.

BELLE NORMANDE, H. P.; flowers pale rose, shaded with silvery white; very large and full; form globular; growth vigorous; of the race of *La Reine*.

BELLE ROSE, H. P.; flowers bright rose, very large, full, and of fine globular form; very sweet; habit good; growth vigorous.

CAPITAINE ROGNAT, H. P.; flowers brilliant red; cupped, large and full; growth vigorous.

CHARLES MARGOTTIN, H. P.; flowers brilliant carmine, their centre fiery red, very large, full, and sweet; form fine; outer petals large and round; growth vigorous; of the race of *Jules Margottin*.

CHARLES WOOD, H. P.; flowers deep red, shaded with blackish-crimson; very large, full, and of fine form; growth vigorous.

CLIMBING DEVONIENSIS, T.; identical with the old *Devoniensis* in flower, but of a rapid running growth, and hence valuable as a climber.

COMTESSE DE PARIS, H. P.; beautiful, distinct lively rose, with lighter edges; flowers very large and double; habit vigorous; a very beautiful variety.

DENIS HELYE, H. P.; flowers brilliant rosy-carmine; lovely color; very large and full; very effective; growth vigorous.

DR. ANDRY, H. P.; flowers dark bright-red; very large, full, and perfectly imbricated; growth vigorous.

DUCHESSE DE CAYLUS, H. P.; flowers brilliant carmine; large, full, and of perfect form; growth vigorous; foliage very rich and fine.

DUCHESSE DE MEDINA CŒLI, H. P.; flowers dark blood-purple; large, full, good, and distinct; growth vigorous.

DUKE OF WELLINGTON, H. P.; flowers bright velvety-red, shaded with blackish-maroon; their centre fiery red; large and full; growth vigorous.

ELIZABETH VIGNERON, H. P.; flowers fine rosy-pink, very large and full; in the style of Lælia, but fuller, fresher, and brighter in color; constitution hardy; growth vigorous.

GÉNÉRAL D'HAUTPOULT, H. P.; flowers brilliant reddish-scarlet; the centre petals sometimes striped with white; large, full, and of globular form.

GLORY OF WALTHAM, H. P. (*Paul*); flowers rich crimson, very large and full; a seedling from Leveson Gower; larger, brighter, darker, and of better form, than the parent; a superb rose, of hardy, vigorous growth.

JEAN ROSENKRANTZ, H. P.; flowers brilliant coral-red; large, full, and of perfect form; growth vigorous.

JOHN KEYNES, H. P.; flowers bright reddish-scarlet, shaded with maroon; large and full; growth vigorous.

KING'S ACRE, H. P. (*Cranston*); flowers bright vermilion-rose; reverse of petals satiny; large, and of fine cupped form; foliage, rich dark-green; growth vigorous.

MADAME VERSCHAFFELT, H. P.; flowers beautiful delicate rose; large, full, and of fine form; growth vigorous; shoots almost thornless.

MADAME ANDRÉ LEROY, H. P.; flowers salmon-rose; large, very double, form fine; growth vigorous.

MADAME CHARLES, T.; flowers sulphur or yellow, their centre salmon; large, full, of good form, and very abundant; growth vigorous; of the race of *Madame Damaizin*.

MADAME CHARLES VERDIER, H. P.; flowers fine vermeil-rose; very large, full, and of fine form; growth vigorous.

MADAME ÉLISE VILMORIN, H. P.; flowers dark vermilion, shaded with blackish-crimson; large, full, of good form, and very abundant; growth vigorous.

MADAME ÉMILE BOYAU, H. P.; flowers soft, rosy flesh-color, changing to blush; sufficiently large, perfect in form, moderate in growth, hardy in constitution; good and distinct.

MADAME GUSTAVE BONNET, B.; flowers white, shaded with rose and carmine; of medium size, full, very abundant, form globular; growth vigorous.

MADAME HERMAN STENGER, H. P.; flowers rose, suffused with lilac; their centre shaded with sulphur; large and full; the outer petals large, form cupped; growth vigorous.

MADAME MOREAU, H. P.; flowers brilliant red, shaded with violet; very large, full; outer petals large; very sweet; growth vigorous.

MADAME ROUSSET, H. P.; flowers beautiful pale rose; the reverse of the petals silvery, large, full, finely cupped, and good habit; growth vigorous.

MADEMOISELLE AMELIE HALPHEN, H. P.; flowers fine rosy-carmine; large, full, of fine form, bright and beautiful; habit good; growth vigorous.

MADEMOISELLE LOIDE DE FALLOUX, H. P.; white, suffused or veined with rose; flowers large, double, and of good form; habit vigorous.

MARÉCHAL NIEL, T.; flowers beautiful deep-yellow; large, full, and of globular form, very sweet; growth vigorous; the shoots well clothed with large shining leaves.

MARGUERITE BONNET, B.; flowers white, shaded with flesh-color; large, full, and of fine form; growth vigorous; of the race of *Louise Odier*.

MARGUERITE DE ST. AMAND, H. P.; flowers rosy flesh-color; large, full, of fine form, and abundant; habit fine; growth vigorous; of the race of *Jules Margottin*.

MARIE BOISSÉE, H. P.; blush-white in opening, passing to pure white when expanded; flowers double and cup-shaped; habit vigorous; very free-flowering.

MICHEL BONNET, B.; flowers beautiful bright rose; large and full; growth vigorous.

MONSIEUR DE PONTBRIANT, H. P.; flowers dark blackish-crimson, shaded with carmine; very large, full, of good form; growth vigorous.

MONSIEUR ÉDOUARD ORY, H. P.; flowers beautiful vermilion; large, full, and of globular form; fine habit; growth vigorous.

PRINCE DE JOINVILLE, H. P.; flowers light crimson; a fine, large, showy rose, of vigorous and hardy habit.

PRINCE EUGÈNE BEAUHARNAIS, H. P.; flowers brilliant reddish-scarlet, shaded with purple; large and full; form cupped; growth vigorous.

PRINCE NAPOLÉON, H. P.; flowers bright rose; very large and very double; growth vigorous; very effective.

PRINCESS LICHTENSTEIN, H. P.; flowers white, globular, large and full; a good hardy, white rose, of compact growth, flowering abundantly.

ROSA MUNDI, H. P.; pure rose, flowers large, double, globular, and well-shaped; habit vigorous.

RUSHTON RADCLYFFE, H. P.; flowers beautiful clear bright red; large, full, and of perfect form; growth vigorous.

SEMIRAMIS, H. P.; flowers clear pink; large, full, and of fine globular form; growth vigorous.

SOUVENIR DE BERNARDIN DE ST. PIERRE, H. P.; flowers varying from crimson to violet; their centre fiery red; large, full, and of fine form; habit good; growth vigorous.
SOUVENIR DE LOUIS GAUDIN, B.; flowers fine reddish-purple, shaded with black; of medium size, full; very abundant; form fine.
SOUVENIR DE WILLIAM WOOD, H. P.; flowers dark blackish-purple, shaded with scarlet; darker than *Prince Camille de Rohan;* large, full, and very effective; growth vigorous.
TRIOMPHE DE LA TERRE DES ROSES, H. P.; flowers fine violet-rose; very large and full; very sweet; blooms freely.
TRIOMPHE DES FRANÇAIS, H. P.; flowers brilliant crimson; large; very double; growth vigorous; fine habit; very free and effective.
WILLIAM BULL, H. P.; flowers brilliant cherry-red; large, full, and of fine globular form; growth vigorous.
XAVIER OLIBO, H. P.; flowers velvety-black, shaded with fiery amaranth; colors exceedingly rich; large; well formed; growth vigorous.

THE END

www.ingramcontent.com/pod-product-compliance
Lightning Source LLC
Chambersburg PA
CBHW021836230426
43669CB00008B/992